Copyright© 2011, 2012 by Nathan Fox

Design by Christopher Imlay

Published by Avocado Books, Los Angeles, California

ISBN: 978-0-9838505-0-2

Cheating the LSAT:
The Fox Test Prep Guide
to a Real LSAT, Vol. 1

by Nathan Fox

For Christine

TABLE OF **CONTENTS**

Fox Test Prep

www.foxtestprep.com
372 West Portal Ave. #4
San Francisco, CA 94127
415-518-0630
fox.edit@gmail.com

CHEATING THE LSAT: THE FOX TEST PREP GUIDE TO A REAL LSAT, VOL. 1

Second Edition

by Nathan Fox

Welcome

(Or: "Cheating the LSAT")

The book you hold in your hands is the distillation of thousands of hours of teaching, studying, and practicing the LSAT. Possessing it confers a blatant and unfair advantage over your competition. Like starting on second base.

Not that scoring from here will be easy. Your performance will be judged relative to the armies of would-be law students who are busy grinding away at study guides and practice LSATs—right this very second. They're meeting in study groups, they're taking prep courses (some good, some terrible), and their parents are writing outsized checks to their private tutors. Like you, they all have jobs and families and all sorts of other responsibilities. But time spent moaning about responsibilities and distractions is time that could better be spent practicing. If you want to go to law school, you first need to strap yourself in and join these people at the grindstone. The LSAT (and law school, and lawyering) will require time, effort, patience, sacrifice, and willpower.

Basically what I'm saying is: GET OUT NOW.

If you're still here, you've decided to join the grinders. And if you're going to join them, you might as well beat them—winning's the fun part.

Most study programs offer quantity over quality: Just bang your head against the wall a million times, and eventually you'll bust through, right? This book is the opposite—it makes efficiency a weapon. The book is written in plain language. It is devoid of trademarked marketing bullshit and unnecessary semantics. It contains no filler and no busywork. Instead, it's a no-nonsense tour of a real LSAT. We've included the questions here as well, so you don't have to bring the test with you to study and keep flipping back and forth. Just grab this book, hit your favorite study place, and you've got everything you need. There are many ways the LSAT tries to eat up your time, but we're going to cheat it out of the opportunity at every turn.

As your tour guide, I'm required to tell you that I'm an expert test-taker who is also an expert teacher. (Any pretense of modesty: shattered!) Question-by-question, you'll see the thought process that leads to one clearly correct answer for (almost) every question. We'll point out the terribly written questions in passing, so you can learn how to stop wasting your time with them. The tour will take about 15 hours to complete, and it will actually be fun. It shouldn't be legal, but it is.

Your unfair advantage starts here.

Meet Your Guide

I took the official LSAT in February of 2007, and scored 179. In 2008, I enrolled at UC Hastings College of the Law. It was the best school within biking distance from my home in San Francisco's Mission District. I was 32 years old at the time, and I had no idea what I wanted to do with my life. I already had a Master's degree in journalism. I already had an MBA. I'd already held, hated, and supremely sucked at a succession of jobs.

Now I'm 35. And as I write this introduction—with a beer at hand—my law school career is coming to a close. I will never be a lawyer, and I couldn't be happier about that. Because the same year I started law school, I discovered my true passion and obvious calling in life. It wasn't law. I'm a teacher.

I know it's my calling because, for the first time in my life, I'm doing the thing that 1) I'm good at, 2) I love, and 3) I can get paid for. If this describes you at your current occupation, then please put down this book and walk away from the LSAT. For good. Seriously. Because professionally, that's about as good as it gets.

For the rest of you (and polls would suggest that's most of you), I'll assume you haven't yet found your calling. I'll assume that a J.D. will move you toward your calling, whether as a lawyer or in some other career. For taking the risk, for wanting to better yourself, and for not settling for unhappiness, I commend you. Law may or may not turn out to be your thing. But you'll have no way of knowing until you try.

Thank you for picking up this book. Before we get started, here's how you can reach me:

Cell phone: 415-518-0630

Email: fox.edit@gmail.com

Your questions, comments, and concerns—not just about the LSAT, but about law school and career counseling in general—are the lifeblood of my business. If you've made it this far, then I consider you my student. I wouldn't be here without you. Let me know how I can help.

How to Use
This Book

The fastest way to learn to ride a bike is to crash. A lot. The technique seems mysterious at first. How the hell do the other kids make it look so easy? You skin your knees, you shed a few tears, you get back up, and you try it one more time. And then one day—maybe when you're on the verge of giving up—you don't crash. Suddenly, before you even realize it, you're halfway down the block. You've done it!

And, of course, as soon as you make this realization, you panic and you crash once more.

You never stop crashing, really. But the crashes become less and less frequent, until they're almost nonexistent. You're never a perfect rider, but you never stop getting better. The more you practice, the better you become.

The LSAT is exactly the same. There is no amount of abstract theory that can help you learn. (*The Theory of Bicycle Physics* would be worthless to a kid.) Instead, you need to try, and fail, and learn from your mistakes. That is the purpose of this book, with emphasis on the last part there, of course.

The instructions are simple:
1. **Do one section of the October 2010 LSAT.** Time yourself, 35 minutes per section. When time is up, check your answers.
2. **Read the strategy introduction.** At the beginning of each section, you'll find a brief primer on my general strategies for that set of questions.
3. **Read the explanations.** And not just for the ones you got wrong. The LSAT is notorious for allowing students to choose the right answer for the wrong reasons. The explanations in this book will help you answer future questions with more certainty.
4. **Repeat.**

Don't focus too intently on any one question. Perfection is not a useful, or even reasonable, goal on the LSAT. Time yourself, but remember that most people don't finish each section. Easier questions tend to appear near the beginning of each section, and most people randomly guess on a few questions at the end of each section—there's no penalty for guessing. Focus on repeatedly nailing the easier questions instead of occasionally getting the harder ones correct, because some of the harder ones are so convoluted that little can be gained from studying them, something I'll point out in the explanations.

The goal here is to try to eliminate your repeated, systematic mistakes. Eventually, just like riding a bike, you'll start to get a feel for it.

Until then, put 35 minutes on the clock—and have fun crashing.

THE OCTOBER 2010 LSAT

SECTION I

Time—35 minutes

27 Questions

Directions: Each set of questions in this section is based on a single passage or a pair of passages. The questions are to be answered on the basis of what is <u>stated</u> or <u>implied</u> in the passage or pair of passages. For some of the questions, more than one of the choices could conceivably answer the question. However, you are to choose the <u>best</u> answer; that is, the response that most accurately and completely answers the question, and blacken the corresponding space on your answer sheet.

The Universal Declaration of Human Rights (UDHR), approved by the United Nations General Assembly in 1948, was the first international treaty to expressly affirm universal respect for human rights.
(5) Prior to 1948 no truly international standard of humanitarian beliefs existed. Although Article 1 of the 1945 UN Charter had been written with the express purpose of obligating the UN to "encourage respect for human rights and for fundamental
(10) freedoms for all without distinction as to race, sex, language, or religion," there were members of delegations from various small countries and representatives of several nongovernmental organizations who felt that the language of Article 1
(15) was not strong enough, and that the Charter as a whole did not go far enough in its efforts to guarantee basic human rights. This group lobbied vigorously to strengthen the Charter's human rights provisions and proposed that member states be
(20) required "to take separate and joint action and to co-operate with the organization for the promotion of human rights." This would have implied an obligation for member states to act on human rights issues. Ultimately, this proposal and others like it were not
(25) adopted; instead, the UDHR was commissioned and drafted.

The original mandate for producing the document was given to the UN Commission on Human Rights in February 1946. Between that time and the General
(30) Assembly's final approval of the document, the UDHR passed through an elaborate eight-stage drafting process in which it made its way through almost every level of the UN hierarchy. The articles were debated at each stage, and all 30 articles were
(35) argued passionately by delegates representing diverse ideologies, traditions, and cultures. The document as it was finally approved set forth the essential principles of freedom and equality for everyone— regardless of sex, race, color, language, religion,
(40) political or other opinion, national or social origin, property, birth or other status. It also asserted a number of fundamental human rights, including among others the right to work, the right to rest and leisure, and the right to education.
(45) While the UDHR is in many ways a progressive document, it also has weaknesses, the most regrettable of which is its nonbinding legal status. For all its strong language and high ideals, the UDHR remains a resolution of a purely programmatic nature.
(50) Nevertheless, the document has led, even if belatedly, to the creation of legally binding human rights

conventions, and it clearly deserves recognition as an international standard-setting piece of work, as a set of aspirations to which UN member states are
(55) intended to strive, and as a call to arms in the name of humanity, justice, and freedom.

1. By referring to the Universal Declaration of Human Rights as "purely programmatic" (line 49) in nature, the author most likely intends to emphasize

   (A) the likelihood that the document will inspire innovative government programs designed to safeguard human rights
   (B) the ability of the document's drafters to translate abstract ideals into concrete standards
   (C) the compromises that went into producing a version of the document that would garner the approval of all relevant parties
   (D) the fact that the guidelines established by the document are ultimately unenforceable
   (E) the frustration experienced by the document's drafters at stubborn resistance from within the UN hierarchy

2. The author most probably quotes directly from both the UN Charter (lines 8–11) and the proposal mentioned in lines 20–22 for which one of the following reasons?

   (A) to contrast the different definitions of human rights in the two documents
   (B) to compare the strength of the human rights language in the two documents
   (C) to identify a bureaucratic vocabulary that is common to the two documents
   (D) to highlight what the author believes to be the most important point in each document
   (E) to call attention to a significant difference in the prose styles of the two documents

3. The author's stance toward the Universal Declaration of Human Rights can best be described as

   (A) unbridled enthusiasm
   (B) qualified approval
   (C) absolute neutrality
   (D) reluctant rejection
   (E) strong hostility

GO ON TO THE NEXT PAGE.

4. According to the passage, each of the following is true of the Universal Declaration of Human Rights EXCEPT:

   (A) It asserts a right to rest and leisure.
   (B) It was drafted after the UN Charter was drafted.
   (C) The UN Commission on Human Rights was charged with producing it.
   (D) It has had no practical consequences.
   (E) It was the first international treaty to explicitly affirm universal respect for human rights.

5. The author would be most likely to agree with which one of the following statements?

   (A) The human rights language contained in Article 1 of the UN Charter is so ambiguous as to be almost wholly ineffectual.
   (B) The weaknesses of the Universal Declaration of Human Rights generally outweigh the strengths of the document.
   (C) It was relatively easy for the drafters of the Universal Declaration of Human Rights to reach a consensus concerning the contents of the document.
   (D) The drafters of the Universal Declaration of Human Rights omitted important rights that should be included in a truly comprehensive list of basic human rights.
   (E) The Universal Declaration of Human Rights would be truer to the intentions of its staunchest proponents if UN member countries were required by law to abide by its provisions.

6. Suppose that a group of independent journalists has uncovered evidence of human rights abuses being perpetrated by a security agency of a UN member state upon a group of political dissidents. Which one of the following approaches to the situation would most likely be advocated by present-day delegates who share the views of the delegates and representatives mentioned in lines 11–14?

   (A) The UN General Assembly authenticates the evidence and then insists upon prompt remedial action on the part of the government of the member state.
   (B) The UN General Assembly stipulates that any proposed response must be unanimously accepted by member states before it can be implemented.
   (C) The UN issues a report critical of the actions of the member state in question and calls for a censure vote in the General Assembly.
   (D) The situation is regarded by the UN as an internal matter that is best left to the discretion of the government of the member state.
   (E) The situation is investigated further by nongovernmental humanitarian organizations that promise to disclose their findings to the public via the international media.

GO ON TO THE NEXT PAGE.

It is commonly assumed that even if some forgeries have aesthetic merit, no forgery has as much as an original by the imitated artist would. Yet even the most prominent art specialists can be duped by a (5) talented artist turned forger into mistaking an almost perfect forgery for an original. For instance, artist Han van Meegeren's *The Disciples at Emmaus* (1937)—painted under the forged signature of the acclaimed Dutch master Jan Vermeer (1632–1675)— (10) attracted lavish praise from experts as one of Vermeer's finest works. The painting hung in a Rotterdam museum until 1945, when, to the great embarrassment of the critics, van Meegeren revealed its origin. Astonishingly, there was at least one highly (15) reputed critic who persisted in believing it to be a Vermeer even after van Meegeren's confession.

Given the experts' initial enthusiasm, some philosophers argue that van Meegeren's painting must have possessed aesthetic characteristics that, in a (20) Vermeer original, would have justified the critics' plaudits. Van Meegeren's *Emmaus* thus raises difficult questions regarding the status of superbly executed forgeries. Is a forgery inherently inferior as art? How are we justified, if indeed we are, in revising (25) downwards our critical assessment of a work unmasked as a forgery? Philosopher of art Alfred Lessing proposes convincing answers to these questions.

A forged work is indeed inferior as art, Lessing (30) argues, but not because of a shortfall in aesthetic qualities strictly defined, that is to say, in the qualities perceptible on the picture's surface. For example, in its composition, its technique, and its brilliant use of color, van Meegeren's work is flawless, even (35) beautiful. Lessing argues instead that the deficiency lies in what might be called the painting's intangible qualities. All art, explains Lessing, involves technique, but not all art involves origination of a new vision, and originality of vision is one of the (40) fundamental qualities by which artistic, as opposed to purely aesthetic, accomplishment is measured. Thus Vermeer is acclaimed for having inaugurated, in the seventeenth century, a new way of seeing, and for pioneering techniques for embodying this new way of (45) seeing through distinctive treatment of light, color, and form.

Even if we grant that van Meegeren, with his undoubted mastery of Vermeer's innovative techniques, produced an aesthetically superior (50) painting, he did so about three centuries after Vermeer developed the techniques in question. Whereas Vermeer's origination of these techniques in the seventeenth century represents a truly impressive and historic achievement, van Meegeren's production (55) of *The Disciples at Emmaus* in the twentieth century presents nothing new or creative to the history of art. Van Meegeren's forgery therefore, for all its aesthetic merits, lacks the historical significance that makes Vermeer's work artistically great.

7. Which one of the following most accurately expresses the main point of the passage?

(A) *The Disciples at Emmaus*, van Meegeren's forgery of a Vermeer, was a failure in both aesthetic and artistic terms.

(B) The aesthetic value of a work of art is less dependent on the work's visible characteristics than on certain intangible characteristics.

(C) Forged artworks are artistically inferior to originals because artistic value depends in large part on originality of vision.

(D) The most skilled forgers can deceive even highly qualified art experts into accepting their work as original.

(E) Art critics tend to be unreliable judges of the aesthetic and artistic quality of works of art.

8. The passage provides the strongest support for inferring that Lessing holds which one of the following views?

(A) The judgments of critics who pronounced *The Disciples at Emmaus* to be aesthetically superb were not invalidated by the revelation that the painting is a forgery.

(B) The financial value of a work of art depends more on its purely aesthetic qualities than on its originality.

(C) Museum curators would be better off not taking art critics' opinions into account when attempting to determine whether a work of art is authentic.

(D) Because it is such a skilled imitation of Vermeer, *The Disciples at Emmaus* is as artistically successful as are original paintings by artists who are less significant than Vermeer.

(E) Works of art that have little or no aesthetic value can still be said to be great achievements in artistic terms.

9. In the first paragraph, the author refers to a highly reputed critic's persistence in believing van Meegeren's forgery to be a genuine Vermeer primarily in order to

(A) argue that many art critics are inflexible in their judgments

(B) indicate that the critics who initially praised *The Disciples at Emmaus* were not as knowledgeable as they appeared

(C) suggest that the painting may yet turn out to be a genuine Vermeer

(D) emphasize that the concept of forgery itself is internally incoherent

(E) illustrate the difficulties that skillfully executed forgeries can pose for art critics

GO ON TO THE NEXT PAGE.

10. The reaction described in which one of the following scenarios is most analogous to the reaction of the art critics mentioned in line 13?

(A) lovers of a musical group contemptuously reject a tribute album recorded by various other musicians as a second-rate imitation

(B) art historians extol the work of a little-known painter as innovative until it is discovered that the painter lived much more recently than was originally thought

(C) diners at a famous restaurant effusively praise the food as delicious until they learn that the master chef is away for the night

(D) literary critics enthusiastically applaud a new novel until its author reveals that its central symbols are intended to represent political views that the critics dislike

(E) movie fans evaluate a particular movie more favorably than they otherwise might have because their favorite actor plays the lead role

11. The passage provides the strongest support for inferring that Lessing holds which one of the following views?

(A) It is probable that many paintings currently hanging in important museums are actually forgeries.

(B) The historical circumstances surrounding the creation of a work are important in assessing the artistic value of that work.

(C) The greatness of an innovative artist depends on how much influence he or she has on other artists.

(D) The standards according to which a work is judged to be a forgery tend to vary from one historical period to another.

(E) An artist who makes use of techniques developed by others cannot be said to be innovative.

12. The passage most strongly supports which one of the following statements?

(A) In any historical period, the criteria by which a work is classified as a forgery can be a matter of considerable debate.

(B) An artist who uses techniques that others have developed is most likely a forger.

(C) A successful forger must originate a new artistic vision.

(D) Works of art created early in the career of a great artist are more likely than those created later to embody historic innovations.

(E) A painting can be a forgery even if it is not a copy of a particular original work of art.

13. Which one of the following, if true, would most strengthen Lessing's contention that a painting can display aesthetic excellence without possessing an equally high degree of artistic value?

(A) Many of the most accomplished art forgers have had moderately successful careers as painters of original works.

(B) Reproductions painted by talented young artists whose traditional training consisted in the copying of masterpieces were often seen as beautiful, but never regarded as great art.

(C) While experts can detect most forgeries, they can be duped by a talented forger who knows exactly what characteristics experts expect to find in the work of a particular painter.

(D) Most attempts at art forgery are ultimately unsuccessful because the forger has not mastered the necessary techniques.

(E) The criteria by which aesthetic excellence is judged change significantly from one century to another and from one culture to another.

GO ON TO THE NEXT PAGE.

Passage A

One function of language is to influence others' behavior by changing what they know, believe, or desire. For humans engaged in conversation, the perception of another's mental state is perhaps the
(5) most common vocalization stimulus.

While animal vocalizations may have evolved because they can potentially alter listeners' behavior to the signaler's benefit, such communication is—in contrast to human language—inadvertent, because
(10) most animals, with the possible exception of chimpanzees, cannot attribute mental states to others. The male *Physalaemus* frog calls because calling causes females to approach and other males to retreat, but there is no evidence that he does so because he attributes knowledge
(15) or desire to other frogs, or because he knows his calls will affect their knowledge and that this knowledge will, in turn, affect their behavior. Research also suggests that, in marked contrast to humans, nonhuman primates do not produce vocalizations in response to perception
(20) of another's need for information. Macaques, for example, give alarm calls when predators approach and coo calls upon finding food, yet experiments reveal no evidence that individuals were more likely to call about these events when they were aware of them but their offspring
(25) were clearly ignorant; similarly, chimpanzees do not appear to adjust their calling to inform ignorant individuals of their own location or that of food. Many animal vocalizations whose production initially seems goal-directed are not as purposeful as they first appear.

Passage B

(30) Many scientists distinguish animal communication systems from human language on the grounds that the former are rigid responses to stimuli, whereas human language is spontaneous and creative.

In this connection, it is commonly stated that no
(35) animal can use its communication system to lie. Obviously, a lie requires intention to deceive: to judge whether a particular instance of animal communication is truly prevarication requires knowledge of the animal's intentions. Language philosopher H. P. Grice explains
(40) that for an individual to mean something by uttering *x*, the individual must intend, in expressing *x*, to induce an audience to believe something and must also intend the utterance to be recognized as so intended. But conscious intention is a category of mental experience
(45) widely believed to be uniquely human. Philosopher Jacques Maritain's discussion of the honeybee's elaborate "waggle-dance" exemplifies this view. Although bees returning to the hive communicate to other bees the distance and direction of food sources,
(50) such communication is, Maritain asserts, merely a conditioned reflex: animals may use communicative signs but lack conscious intention regarding their use.

But these arguments are circular: conscious intention is ruled out a priori and then its absence
(55) taken as evidence that animal communication is fundamentally different from human language. In fact, the narrowing of the perceived gap between animal communication and human language revealed by recent research with chimpanzees and other animals
(60) calls into question not only the assumption that the difference between animal and human communication is qualitative rather than merely quantitative, but also the accompanying assumption that animals respond mechanically to stimuli, whereas humans speak with
(65) conscious understanding and intent.

14. Both passages are primarily concerned with addressing which one of the following questions?

(A) Are animals capable of deliberately prevaricating in order to achieve specific goals?

(B) Are the communications of animals characterized by conscious intention?

(C) What kinds of stimuli are most likely to elicit animal vocalizations?

(D) Are the communication systems of nonhuman primates qualitatively different from those of all other animals?

(E) Is there a scientific consensus about the differences between animal communication systems and human language?

15. In discussing the philosopher Maritain, the author of passage B seeks primarily to

(A) describe an interpretation of animal communication that the author believes rests on a logical error

(B) suggest by illustration that there is conscious intention underlying the communicative signs employed by certain animals

(C) present an argument in support of the view that animal communication systems are spontaneous and creative

(D) furnish specific evidence against the theory that most animal communication is merely a conditioned reflex

(E) point to a noted authority on animal communication whose views the author regards with respect

GO ON TO THE NEXT PAGE.

16. The author of passage B would be most likely to agree with which one of the following statements regarding researchers who subscribe to the position articulated in passage A?

    (A) They fail to recognize that humans often communicate without any clear idea of their listeners' mental states.
    (B) Most of them lack the credentials needed to assess the relevant experimental evidence correctly.
    (C) They ignore well-known evidence that animals do in fact practice deception.
    (D) They make assumptions about matters that should be determined empirically.
    (E) They falsely believe that all communication systems can be explained in terms of their evolutionary benefits.

17. Which one of the following assertions from passage A provides support for the view attributed to Maritain in passage B (lines 50–52)?

    (A) One function of language is to influence the behavior of others by changing what they think.
    (B) Animal vocalizations may have evolved because they have the potential to alter listeners' behavior to the signaler's benefit.
    (C) It is possible that chimpanzees may have the capacity to attribute mental states to others.
    (D) There is no evidence that the male *Physalaemus* frog calls because he knows that his calls will affect the knowledge of other frogs.
    (E) Macaques give alarm calls when predators approach and coo calls upon finding food.

18. The authors would be most likely to disagree over

    (A) the extent to which communication among humans involves the ability to perceive the mental states of others
    (B) the importance of determining to what extent animal communication systems differ from human language
    (C) whether human language and animal communication differ from one another qualitatively or merely in a matter of degree
    (D) whether chimpanzees' vocalizations suggest that they may possess the capacity to attribute mental states to others
    (E) whether animals' vocalizations evolved to alter the behavior of other animals in a way that benefits the signaler

19. Passage B differs from passage A in that passage B is more

    (A) optimistic regarding the ability of science to answer certain fundamental questions
    (B) disapproving of the approach taken by others writing on the same general topic
    (C) open-minded in its willingness to accept the validity of apparently conflicting positions
    (D) supportive of ongoing research related to the question at hand
    (E) circumspect in its refusal to commit itself to any positions with respect to still-unsettled research questions

GO ON TO THE NEXT PAGE.

In contrast to the mainstream of U.S. historiography during the late nineteenth and early twentieth centuries, African American historians of the period, such as George Washington Williams and
(5) W. E. B. DuBois, adopted a transnational perspective. This was true for several reasons, not the least of which was the necessity of doing so if certain aspects of the history of African Americans in the United States were to be treated honestly.
(10) First, there was the problem of citizenship. Even after the adoption in 1868 of the Fourteenth Amendment to the U.S. Constitution, which defined citizenship, the question of citizenship for African Americans had not been genuinely resolved. Because
(15) of this, emigrationist sentiment was a central issue in black political discourse, and both issues were critical topics for investigation. The implications for historical scholarship and national identity were enormous. While some black leaders insisted on their right to U.S.
(20) citizenship, others called on black people to emigrate and find a homeland of their own. Most African Americans were certainly not willing to relinquish their claims to the benefits of U.S. citizenship, but many had reached a point of profound pessimism and had
(25) begun to question their allegiance to the United States.
Mainstream U.S. historiography was firmly rooted in a nationalist approach during this period; the glorification of the nation and a focus on the nation-state as a historical force were dominant. The
(30) expanding spheres of influence of Europe and the United States prompted the creation of new genealogies of nations, new myths about the inevitability of nations, their "temperaments," their destinies. African American intellectuals who
(35) confronted the nationalist approach to historiography were troubled by its implications. Some argued that imperialism was a natural outgrowth of nationalism and its view that a state's strength is measured by the extension of its political power over colonial territory;
(40) the scramble for colonial empires was a distinct aspect of nationalism in the latter part of the nineteenth century.
Yet, for all their distrust of U.S. nationalism, most early black historians were themselves engaged in a
(45) sort of nation building. Deliberately or not, they contributed to the formation of a collective identity, reconstructing a glorious African past for the purposes of overturning degrading representations of blackness and establishing a firm cultural basis for a
(50) shared identity. Thus, one might argue that black historians' internationalism was a manifestation of a kind of nationalism that posits a diasporic community, which, while lacking a sovereign territory or official language, possesses a single culture, however
(55) mythical, with singular historical roots. Many members of this diaspora saw themselves as an oppressed "nation" without a homeland, or they imagined Africa as home. Hence, these historians understood their task to be the writing of the history
(60) of a people scattered by force and circumstance, a history that began in Africa.

20. Which one of the following most accurately expresses the main idea of the passage?

(A) Historians are now recognizing that the major challenge faced by African Americans in the late nineteenth and early twentieth centuries was the struggle for citizenship.

(B) Early African American historians who practiced a transnational approach to history were primarily interested in advancing an emigrationist project.

(C) U.S. historiography in the late nineteenth and early twentieth centuries was characterized by a conflict between African American historians who viewed history from a transnational perspective and mainstream historians who took a nationalist perspective.

(D) The transnational perspective of early African American historians countered mainstream nationalist historiography, but it was arguably nationalist itself to the extent that it posited a culturally unified diasporic community.

(E) Mainstream U.S. historians in the late nineteenth and early twentieth centuries could no longer justify their nationalist approach to history once they were confronted with the transnational perspective taken by African American historians.

21. Which one of the following phrases most accurately conveys the sense of the word "reconstructing" as it is used in line 47?

(A) correcting a misconception about
(B) determining the sequence of events in
(C) investigating the implications of
(D) rewarding the promoters of
(E) shaping a conception of

22. Which one of the following is most strongly supported by the passage?

(A) Emigrationist sentiment would not have been as strong among African Americans in the late nineteenth century had the promise of U.S. citizenship been fully realized for African Americans at that time.

(B) Scholars writing the history of diasporic communities generally do not discuss the forces that initially caused the scattering of the members of those communities.

(C) Most historians of the late nineteenth and early twentieth centuries endeavored to make the histories of the nations about which they wrote seem more glorious than they actually were.

(D) To be properly considered nationalist, a historical work must ignore the ways in which one nation's foreign policy decisions affected other nations.

(E) A considerable number of early African American historians embraced nationalism and the inevitability of the dominance of the nation-state.

GO ON TO THE NEXT PAGE.

23. As it is described in the passage, the transnational approach employed by African American historians working in the late nineteenth and early twentieth centuries would be best exemplified by a historical study that

  (A) investigated the extent to which European and U.S. nationalist mythologies contradicted one another

  (B) defined the national characters of the United States and several European nations by focusing on their treatment of minority populations rather than on their territorial ambitions

  (C) recounted the attempts by the United States to gain control over new territories during the late nineteenth and early twentieth centuries

  (D) considered the impact of emigrationist sentiment among African Americans on U.S. foreign policy in Africa during the late nineteenth century

  (E) examined the extent to which African American culture at the turn of the century incorporated traditions that were common to a number of African cultures

24. The passage provides information sufficient to answer which one of the following questions?

  (A) Which African nations did early African American historians research in writing their histories of the African diaspora?

  (B) What were some of the African languages spoken by the ancestors of the members of the African diasporic community who were living in the United States in the late nineteenth century?

  (C) Over which territories abroad did the United States attempt to extend its political power in the latter part of the nineteenth century?

  (D) Are there textual ambiguities in the Fourteenth Amendment that spurred the conflict over U.S. citizenship for African Americans?

  (E) In what ways did African American leaders respond to the question of citizenship for African Americans in the latter part of the nineteenth century?

25. The author of the passage would be most likely to agree with which one of the following statements?

  (A) Members of a particular diasporic community have a common country of origin.

  (B) Territorial sovereignty is not a prerequisite for the project of nation building.

  (C) Early African American historians who rejected nationalist historiography declined to engage in historical myth-making of any kind.

  (D) The most prominent African American historians in the late nineteenth and early twentieth centuries advocated emigration for African Americans.

  (E) Historians who employed a nationalist approach focused on entirely different events from those studied and written about by early African American historians.

26. The main purpose of the second paragraph of the passage is to

  (A) explain why early African American historians felt compelled to approach historiography in the way that they did

  (B) show that governmental actions such as constitutional amendments do not always have the desired effect

  (C) support the contention that African American intellectuals in the late nineteenth century were critical of U.S. imperialism

  (D) establish that some African American political leaders in the late nineteenth century advocated emigration as an alternative to fighting for the benefits of U.S. citizenship

  (E) argue that the definition of citizenship contained in the Fourteenth Amendment to the U.S. Constitution is too limited

27. As it is presented in the passage, the approach to history taken by mainstream U.S. historians of the late nineteenth and early twentieth centuries is most similar to the approach exemplified in which one of the following?

  (A) An elected official writes a memo suggesting that because a particular course of action has been successful in the past, the government should continue to pursue that course of action.

  (B) A biographer of a famous novelist argues that the precocity apparent in certain of the novelist's early achievements confirms that her success was attributable to innate talent.

  (C) A doctor maintains that because a certain medication was developed expressly for the treatment of an illness, it is the best treatment for that illness.

  (D) A newspaper runs a series of articles in order to inform the public about the environmentally hazardous practices of a large corporation.

  (E) A scientist gets the same result from an experiment several times and therefore concludes that its chemical reactions always proceed in the observed fashion.

S T O P

IF YOU FINISH BEFORE TIME IS CALLED, YOU MAY CHECK YOUR WORK ON THIS SECTION ONLY.
DO NOT WORK ON ANY OTHER SECTION IN THE TEST.

SECTION II

Time—35 minutes

25 Questions

<u>Directions:</u> The questions in this section are based on the reasoning contained in brief statements or passages. For some questions, more than one of the choices could conceivably answer the question. However, you are to choose the <u>best</u> answer; that is, the response that most accurately and completely answers the question. You should not make assumptions that are by commonsense standards implausible, superfluous, or incompatible with the passage. After you have chosen the best answer, blacken the corresponding space on your answer sheet.

1. Mary to Jamal: You acknowledge that as the legitimate owner of this business I have the legal right to sell it whenever I wish. But also you claim that because loyal employees will suffer if I sell it, I therefore have no right to do so. Obviously, your statements taken together are absurd.

    Mary's reasoning is most vulnerable to the criticism that she

    (A) overlooks the possibility that when Jamal claims that she has no right to sell the business, he simply means she has no right to do so at this time
    (B) overlooks the possibility that her employees also have rights related to the sale of the business
    (C) provides no evidence for the claim that she does have a right to sell the business
    (D) overlooks the possibility that Jamal is referring to two different kinds of right
    (E) attacks Jamal's character rather than his argument

2. Since there is no survival value in an animal's having an organ that is able to function when all its other organs have broken down to such a degree that the animal dies, it is a result of the efficiency of natural selection that no organ is likely to evolve in such a way that it greatly outlasts the body's other organs.

    Of the following, which one illustrates a principle that is most similar to the principle illustrated by the passage?

    (A) A store in a lower-income neighborhood finds that it is unable to sell its higher-priced goods and so stocks them only when ordered by a customer.
    (B) The body of an animal with a deficient organ is often able to compensate for that deficiency when other organs perform the task the deficient one normally performs.
    (C) One car model produced by an automobile manufacturer has a life expectancy that is so much longer than its other models that its great popularity requires the manufacturer to stop producing some of the other models.
    (D) Athletes occasionally overdevelop some parts of their bodies to such a great extent that other parts of their bodies are more prone to injury as a result.
    (E) Automotive engineers find that it is not cost-effective to manufacture a given automobile part of such high quality that it outlasts all other parts of the automobile, as doing so would not raise the overall quality of the automobile.

GO ON TO THE NEXT PAGE.

3. Commentator: If a political administration is both economically successful and successful at protecting individual liberties, then it is an overall success. Even an administration that fails to care for the environment may succeed overall if it protects individual liberties. So far, the present administration has not cared for the environment but has successfully protected individual liberties.

If all of the statements above are true, then which one of the following must be true?

(A) The present administration is economically successful.

(B) The present administration is not an overall success.

(C) If the present administration is economically successful, then it is an overall success.

(D) If the present administration had been economically successful, it would have cared for the environment.

(E) If the present administration succeeds at environmental protection, then it will be an overall success.

4. The legislature is considering a proposed bill that would prohibit fishing in Eagle Bay. Despite widespread concern over the economic effect this ban would have on the local fishing industry, the bill should be enacted. The bay has one of the highest water pollution levels in the nation, and a recent study of the bay's fish found that 80 percent of them contained toxin levels that exceed governmental safety standards. Continuing to permit fishing in Eagle Bay could thus have grave effects on public health.

The argument proceeds by presenting evidence that

(A) the toxic contamination of fish in Eagle Bay has had grave economic effects on the local fishing industry

(B) the moral principle that an action must be judged on the basis of its foreseeable effects is usually correct

(C) the opponents of the ban have failed to weigh properly its foreseeable negative effects against its positive ones

(D) failure to enact the ban would carry with it unacceptable risks for the public welfare

(E) the ban would reduce the level of toxins in the fish in Eagle Bay

5. Vandenburg: This art museum is not adhering to its purpose. Its founders intended it to devote as much attention to contemporary art as to the art of earlier periods, but its collection of contemporary art is far smaller than its other collections.

Simpson: The relatively small size of the museum's contemporary art collection is appropriate. It's an art museum, not an ethnographic museum designed to collect every style of every period. Its contemporary art collection is small because its curators believe that there is little high-quality contemporary art.

Which one of the following principles, if valid, most helps to justify the reasoning in Simpson's response to Vandenburg?

(A) An art museum should collect only works that its curators consider to be of high artistic quality.

(B) An art museum should not collect any works that violate the purpose defined by the museum's founders.

(C) An art museum's purpose need not be to collect every style of every period.

(D) An ethnographic museum's purpose should be defined according to its curators' beliefs.

(E) The intentions of an art museum's curators should not determine what is collected by that museum.

6. Over the last five years, every new major alternative-energy initiative that initially was promised government funding has since seen that funding severely curtailed. In no such case has the government come even close to providing the level of funds initially earmarked for these projects. Since large corporations have made it a point to discourage alternative-energy projects, it is likely that the corporations' actions influenced the government's funding decisions.

Which one of the following, if true, most strengthens the reasoning above?

(A) For the past two decades, most alternative-energy initiatives have received little or no government funding.

(B) The funding initially earmarked for a government project is always subject to change, given the mechanisms by which the political process operates.

(C) The only research projects whose government funding has been severely curtailed are those that large corporations have made it a point to discourage.

(D) Some projects encouraged by large corporations have seen their funding severely curtailed over the last five years.

(E) All large corporations have made it a point to discourage some forms of research.

GO ON TO THE NEXT PAGE.

7. Talbert: Chess is beneficial for school-age children. It is enjoyable, encourages foresight and logical thinking, and discourages carelessness, inattention, and impulsiveness. In short, it promotes mental maturity.

   Sklar: My objection to teaching chess to children is that it diverts mental activity from something with societal value, such as science, into something that has no societal value.

   Talbert's and Sklar's statements provide the strongest support for holding that they disagree with each other over whether

   (A) chess promotes mental maturity
   (B) many activities promote mental maturity just as well as chess does
   (C) chess is socially valuable and science is not
   (D) children should be taught to play chess
   (E) children who neither play chess nor study science are mentally immature

8. Marcia: Not all vegetarian diets lead to nutritional deficiencies. Research shows that vegetarians can obtain a full complement of proteins and minerals from nonanimal foods.

   Theodora: You are wrong in claiming that vegetarianism cannot lead to nutritional deficiencies. If most people became vegetarians, some of those losing jobs due to the collapse of many meat-based industries would fall into poverty and hence be unable to afford a nutritionally adequate diet.

   Theodora's reply to Marcia's argument is most vulnerable to criticism on the grounds that her reply

   (A) is directed toward disproving a claim that Marcia did not make
   (B) ignores the results of the research cited by Marcia
   (C) takes for granted that no meat-based industries will collapse unless most people become vegetarians
   (D) uses the word "diet" in a nontechnical sense whereas Marcia's argument uses this term in a medical sense
   (E) takes for granted that people losing jobs in meat-based industries would become vegetarians

9. Musicologist: Classification of a musical instrument depends on the mechanical action through which it produces music. So the piano is properly called a percussion instrument, not a stringed instrument. Even though the vibration of the piano's strings is what makes its sound, the strings are caused to vibrate by the impact of hammers.

   Which one of the following most accurately expresses the main conclusion of the musicologist's argument?

   (A) Musical instruments should be classified according to the mechanical actions through which they produce sound.
   (B) Musical instruments should not be classified based on the way musicians interact with them.
   (C) Some people classify the piano as a stringed instrument because of the way the piano produces sound.
   (D) The piano should be classified as a stringed instrument rather than as a percussion instrument.
   (E) It is correct to classify the piano as a percussion instrument rather than as a stringed instrument.

10. In a vast ocean region, phosphorus levels have doubled in the past few decades due to agricultural runoff pouring out of a large river nearby. The phosphorus stimulates the growth of plankton near the ocean surface. Decaying plankton fall to the ocean floor, where bacteria devour them, consuming oxygen in the process. Due to the resulting oxygen depletion, few fish can survive in this region.

    Which one of the following can be properly inferred from the information above?

    (A) The agricultural runoff pouring out of the river contributes to the growth of plankton near the ocean surface.
    (B) Before phosphorus levels doubled in the ocean region, most fish were able to survive in that region.
    (C) If agricultural runoff ceased pouring out of the river, there would be no bacteria on the ocean floor devouring decaying plankton.
    (D) The quantity of agricultural runoff pouring out of the river has doubled in the past few decades.
    (E) The amount of oxygen in a body of water is in general inversely proportional to the level of phosphorus in that body of water.

GO ON TO THE NEXT PAGE.

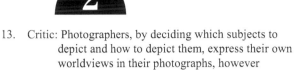

11. Psychologists observing a shopping mall parking lot found that, on average, drivers spent 39 seconds leaving a parking space when another car was quietly waiting to enter it, 51 seconds if the driver of the waiting car honked impatiently, but only 32 seconds leaving a space when no one was waiting. This suggests that drivers feel possessive of their parking spaces even when leaving them, and that this possessiveness increases in reaction to indications that another driver wants the space.

Which one of the following, if true, most weakens the reasoning?

(A) The more pressure most drivers feel because others are waiting for them to perform maneuvers with their cars, the less quickly they are able to perform them.

(B) The amount of time drivers spend entering a parking space is not noticeably affected by whether other drivers are waiting for them to do so, nor by whether those other drivers are honking impatiently.

(C) It is considerably more difficult and time-consuming for a driver to maneuver a car out of a parking space if another car waiting to enter that space is nearby.

(D) Parking spaces in shopping mall parking lots are unrepresentative of parking spaces in general with respect to the likelihood that other cars will be waiting to enter them.

(E) Almost any driver leaving a parking space will feel angry at another driver who honks impatiently, and this anger will influence the amount of time spent leaving the space.

12. Shark teeth are among the most common vertebrate fossils; yet fossilized shark skeletons are much less common—indeed, comparatively rare among fossilized vertebrate skeletons.

Which one of the following, if true, most helps to resolve the apparent paradox described above?

(A) Unlike the bony skeletons of other vertebrates, shark skeletons are composed of cartilage, and teeth and bone are much more likely to fossilize than cartilage is.

(B) The rare fossilized skeletons of sharks that are found are often found in areas other than those in which fossils of shark teeth are plentiful.

(C) Fossils of sharks' teeth are quite difficult to distinguish from fossils of other kinds of teeth.

(D) Some species of sharks alive today grow and lose many sets of teeth during their lifetimes.

(E) The physical and chemical processes involved in the fossilization of sharks' teeth are as common as those involved in the fossilization of shark skeletons.

13. Critic: Photographers, by deciding which subjects to depict and how to depict them, express their own worldviews in their photographs, however realistically those photographs may represent reality. Thus, photographs are interpretations of reality.

The argument's conclusion is properly drawn if which one of the following is assumed?

(A) Even representing a subject realistically can involve interpreting that subject.

(B) To express a worldview is to interpret reality.

(C) All visual art expresses the artist's worldview.

(D) Any interpretation of reality involves the expression of a worldview.

(E) Nonrealistic photographs, like realistic photographs, express the worldviews of the photographers who take them.

14. Geologists recently discovered marks that closely resemble worm tracks in a piece of sandstone. These marks were made more than half a billion years earlier than the earliest known traces of multicellular animal life. Therefore, the marks are probably the traces of geological processes rather than of worms.

Which one of the following, if true, most weakens the argument?

(A) It is sometimes difficult to estimate the precise age of a piece of sandstone.

(B) Geological processes left a substantial variety of marks in sandstone more than half a billion years before the earliest known multicellular animal life existed.

(C) There were some early life forms other than worms that are known to have left marks that are hard to distinguish from those found in the piece of sandstone.

(D) At the place where the sandstone was found, the only geological processes that are likely to mark sandstone in ways that resemble worm tracks could not have occurred at the time the marks were made.

(E) Most scientists knowledgeable about early animal life believe that worms are likely to have been among the earliest forms of multicellular animal life on Earth, but evidence of their earliest existence is scarce because they are composed solely of soft tissue.

GO ON TO THE NEXT PAGE.

15. Often a type of organ or body structure is the only physically feasible means of accomplishing a given task, so it should be unsurprising if, like eyes or wings, that type of organ or body structure evolves at different times in a number of completely unrelated species. After all, whatever the difference of heritage and habitat, as organisms animals have fundamentally similar needs and so _____.

Which one of the following most logically completes the last sentence of the passage?

(A) will often live in the same environment as other species quite different from themselves

(B) will in many instances evolve similar adaptations enabling them to satisfy these needs

(C) will develop adaptations allowing them to satisfy these needs

(D) will resemble other species having different biological needs

(E) will all develop eyes or wings as adaptations

16. Engineer: Thermophotovoltaic generators are devices that convert heat into electricity. The process of manufacturing steel produces huge amounts of heat that currently go to waste. So if steel-manufacturing plants could feed the heat they produce into thermophotovoltaic generators, they would greatly reduce their electric bills, thereby saving money.

Which one of the following is an assumption on which the engineer's argument depends?

(A) There is no other means of utilizing the heat produced by the steel-manufacturing process that would be more cost effective than installing thermophotovoltaic generators.

(B) Using current technology, it would be possible for steel-manufacturing plants to feed the heat they produce into thermophotovoltaic generators in such a way that those generators could convert at least some of that heat into electricity.

(C) The amount steel-manufacturing plants would save on their electric bills by feeding heat into thermophotovoltaic generators would be sufficient to cover the cost of purchasing and installing those generators.

(D) At least some steel-manufacturing plants rely on electricity as their primary source of energy in the steel-manufacturing process.

(E) There are at least some steel-manufacturing plants that could greatly reduce their electricity bills only if they used some method of converting wasted heat or other energy from the steel-manufacturing process into electricity.

17. Herbalist: While standard antibiotics typically have just one active ingredient, herbal antibacterial remedies typically contain several. Thus, such herbal remedies are more likely to retain their effectiveness against new, resistant strains of bacteria than are standard antibiotics. For a strain of bacteria, the difficulty of developing resistance to an herbal antibacterial remedy is like a cook's difficulty in trying to prepare a single meal that will please all of several dozen guests, a task far more difficult than preparing one meal that will please a single guest.

In the analogy drawn in the argument above, which one of the following corresponds to a standard antibiotic?

(A) a single guest
(B) several dozen guests
(C) the pleasure experienced by a single guest
(D) a cook
(E) the ingredients available to a cook

18. To find out how barn owls learn how to determine the direction from which sounds originate, scientists put distorting lenses over the eyes of young barn owls before the owls first opened their eyes. The owls with these lenses behaved as if objects making sounds were farther to the right than they actually were. Once the owls matured, the lenses were removed, yet the owls continued to act as if they misjudged the location of the source of sounds. The scientists consequently hypothesized that once a barn owl has developed an auditory scheme for estimating the point from which sounds originate, it ceases to use vision to locate sounds.

The scientists' reasoning is vulnerable to which one of the following criticisms?

(A) It fails to consider whether the owls' vision was permanently impaired by their having worn the lenses while immature.

(B) It assumes that the sense of sight is equally good in all owls.

(C) It attributes human reasoning processes to a nonhuman organism.

(D) It neglects to consider how similar distorting lenses might affect the behavior of other bird species.

(E) It uses as evidence experimental results that were irrelevant to the conclusion.

GO ON TO THE NEXT PAGE.

19. As often now as in the past, newspaper journalists use direct or indirect quotation to report unsupported or false claims made by newsmakers. However, journalists are becoming less likely to openly challenge the veracity of such claims within their articles.

Each of the following, if true, helps to explain the trend in journalism described above EXCEPT:

(A) Newspaper publishers have found that many readers will cancel a subscription simply because a view they take for granted has been disputed by the publication.

(B) The areas of knowledge on which journalists report are growing in specialization and diversity, while journalists themselves are not becoming more broadly knowledgeable.

(C) Persons supporting controversial views more and more frequently choose to speak only to reporters who seem sympathetic to their views.

(D) A basic principle of journalism holds that debate over controversial issues draws the attention of the public.

(E) Journalists who challenge the veracity of claims are often criticized for failing their professional obligation to be objective.

20. When people show signs of having a heart attack an electrocardiograph (EKG) is often used to diagnose their condition. In a study, a computer program for EKG diagnosis of heart attacks was pitted against a very experienced, highly skilled cardiologist. The program correctly diagnosed a significantly higher proportion of the cases that were later confirmed to be heart attacks than did the cardiologist. Interpreting EKG data, therefore, should be left to computer programs.

Which one of the following, if true, most weakens the argument?

(A) Experts agreed that the cardiologist made few obvious mistakes in reading and interpreting the EKG data.

(B) The practice of medicine is as much an art as a science, and computer programs are not easily adapted to making subjective judgments.

(C) The cardiologist correctly diagnosed a significantly higher proportion of the cases in which no heart attack occurred than did the computer program.

(D) In a considerable percentage of cases, EKG data alone are insufficient to enable either computer programs or cardiologists to make accurate diagnoses.

(E) The cardiologist in the study was unrepresentative of cardiologists in general with respect to skill and experience.

21. A government study indicates that raising speed limits to reflect the actual average speeds of traffic on level, straight stretches of high-speed roadways reduces the accident rate. Since the actual average speed for level, straight stretches of high-speed roadways tends to be 120 kilometers per hour (75 miles per hour), that should be set as a uniform national speed limit for level, straight stretches of all such roadways.

Which one of the following principles, if valid, most helps to justify the reasoning above?

(A) Uniform national speed limits should apply only to high-speed roadways.

(B) Traffic laws applying to high-speed roadways should apply uniformly across the nation.

(C) A uniform national speed limit for high-speed roadways should be set only if all such roadways have roughly equal average speeds of traffic.

(D) Long-standing laws that are widely violated are probably not good laws.

(E) Any measure that reduces the rate of traffic accidents should be implemented.

GO ON TO THE NEXT PAGE.

22. Psychiatrist: In treating first-year students at this
     university, I have noticed that those reporting the
     highest levels of spending on recreation score at
     about the same level on standard screening
     instruments for anxiety and depression as those
     reporting the lowest levels of spending on
     recreation. This suggests that the first-year
     students with high levels of spending on
     recreation could reduce that spending without
     increasing their anxiety or depression.

Each of the following, if true, strengthens the
psychiatrist's argument EXCEPT:

(A)   At other universities, first-year students
      reporting the highest levels of spending on
      recreation also show the same degree of
      anxiety and depression as do those reporting
      the lowest levels of such spending.
(B)   Screening of first-year students at the university
      who report moderate levels of spending on
      recreation reveals that those students are less
      anxious and depressed than both those with the
      highest and those with the lowest levels of
      spending on recreation.
(C)   Among adults between the ages of 40 and 60,
      increased levels of spending on recreation are
      strongly correlated with decreased levels of
      anxiety and depression.
(D)   The screening instruments used by the
      psychiatrist are extremely accurate in revealing
      levels of anxiety and depression among
      university students.
(E)   Several of the psychiatrist's patients who are
      first-year students at the university have
      reduced their spending on recreation from very
      high levels to very low levels without
      increasing their anxiety or depression.

23. Every brick house on River Street has a front yard.
     Most of the houses on River Street that have front yards
     also have two stories. So most of the brick houses on
     River Street have two stories.

Which one of the following is most appropriate as an
analogy demonstrating that the reasoning in the
argument above is flawed?

(A)   By that line of reasoning, we could conclude
      that most politicians have run for office, since
      all legislators are politicians and most
      legislators have run for office.
(B)   By that line of reasoning, we could conclude
      that most public servants are legislators, since
      most legislators have run for office and most
      politicians who have run for office are public
      servants.
(C)   By that line of reasoning, we could conclude
      that not every public servant has run for office,
      since every legislator is a public servant but
      some public servants are not legislators.
(D)   By that line of reasoning, we could conclude
      that most legislators have never run for office,
      since most public servants have never run for
      office and all legislators are public servants.
(E)   By that line of reasoning, we could conclude
      that most legislators are not public servants,
      since most public servants have not run for
      office and most legislators have run for office.

GO ON TO THE NEXT PAGE.

24. Historian: It is unlikely that someone would see history
       as the working out of moral themes unless he or
       she held clear and unambiguous moral beliefs.
       However, one's inclination to morally judge
       human behavior decreases as one's knowledge of
       history increases. Consequently, the more history
       a person knows, the less likely that person is to
       view history as the working out of moral themes.

The conclusion of the argument is properly drawn if
which one of the following is assumed?

(A)   Historical events that fail to elicit moral
        disapproval are generally not considered to
        exemplify a moral theme.
(B)   The less inclined one is to morally judge human
        behavior, the less likely it is that one holds
        clear and unambiguous moral beliefs.
(C)   Only those who do not understand human
        history attribute moral significance to historical
        events.
(D)   The more clear and unambiguous one's moral
        beliefs, the more likely one is to view history
        as the working out of moral themes.
(E)   People tend to be less objective regarding a
        subject about which they possess extensive
        knowledge than regarding a subject about
        which they do not possess extensive
        knowledge.

25. A recent poll revealed that most students at our
     university prefer that the university, which is searching
     for a new president, hire someone who has extensive
     experience as a university president. However, in the
     very same poll, the person most students chose from
     among a list of leading candidates as the one they
     would most like to see hired was someone who has
     never served as a university president.

Which one of the following, if true, most helps to
account for the apparent discrepancy in the students'
preferences?

(A)   Because several of the candidates listed in the
        poll had extensive experience as university
        presidents, not all of the candidates could be
        differentiated on this basis alone.
(B)   Most of the candidates listed in the poll had
        extensive experience as university presidents.
(C)   Students taking the poll had fewer candidates to
        choose from than were currently being
        considered for the position.
(D)   Most of the students taking the poll did not
        know whether any of the leading candidates
        listed in the poll had ever served as a
        university president.
(E)   Often a person can be well suited to a position
        even though they have relatively little
        experience in such a position.

S T O P

IF YOU FINISH BEFORE TIME IS CALLED, YOU MAY CHECK YOUR WORK ON THIS SECTION ONLY.
DO NOT WORK ON ANY OTHER SECTION IN THE TEST.

SECTION III

Time—35 minutes

23 Questions

<u>Directions:</u> Each group of questions in this section is based on a set of conditions. In answering some of the questions, it may be useful to draw a rough diagram. Choose the response that most accurately and completely answers each question and blacken the corresponding space on your answer sheet.

<u>Questions 1–5</u>

Exactly six workers—Faith, Gus, Hannah, Juan, Kenneth, and Lisa—will travel to a business convention in two cars—car 1 and car 2. Each car must carry at least two of the workers, one of whom will be assigned to drive. For the entire trip, the workers will comply with an assignment that also meets the following constraints:

Either Faith or Gus must drive the car in which Hannah travels.

Either Faith or Kenneth must drive the car in which Juan travels.

Gus must travel in the same car as Lisa.

1. Which one of the following is a possible assignment of the workers to the cars?

   (A) car 1: Faith (driver), Hannah, and Juan
        car 2: Gus (driver), Kenneth, and Lisa
   (B) car 1: Faith (driver), Hannah, and Kenneth
        car 2: Lisa (driver), Gus, and Juan
   (C) car 1: Faith (driver), Juan, Kenneth, and Lisa
        car 2: Gus (driver) and Hannah
   (D) car 1: Faith (driver) and Juan
        car 2: Kenneth (driver), Gus, Hannah, and Lisa
   (E) car 1: Gus (driver), Hannah, and Lisa
        car 2: Juan (driver), Faith, and Kenneth

2. The two workers who drive the cars CANNOT be

   (A) Faith and Gus
   (B) Faith and Kenneth
   (C) Faith and Lisa
   (D) Gus and Kenneth
   (E) Kenneth and Lisa

3. If Lisa drives one of the cars, then which one of the following could be true?

   (A) Faith travels in the same car as Kenneth.
   (B) Faith travels in the same car as Lisa.
   (C) Gus travels in the same car as Hannah.
   (D) Gus travels in the same car as Juan.
   (E) Hannah travels in the same car as Lisa.

4. If Faith travels with two other workers in car 1, and if Faith is not the driver, then the person in car 1 other than Faith and the driver must be

   (A) Gus
   (B) Hannah
   (C) Juan
   (D) Kenneth
   (E) Lisa

5. Which one of the following CANNOT be true?

   (A) Gus is the only person other than the driver in one of the cars.
   (B) Hannah is the only person other than the driver in one of the cars.
   (C) Juan is the only person other than the driver in one of the cars.
   (D) Kenneth is the only person other than the driver in one of the cars.
   (E) Lisa is the only person other than the driver in one of the cars.

GO ON TO THE NEXT PAGE.

Questions 6–11

An archaeologist has six ancient artifacts—a figurine, a headdress, a jar, a necklace, a plaque, and a tureen—no two of which are the same age. She will order them from first (oldest) to sixth (most recent). The following has already been determined:

The figurine is older than both the jar and the headdress.
The necklace and the jar are both older than the tureen.
Either the plaque is older than both the headdress and the necklace, or both the headdress and the necklace are older than the plaque.

6. Which one of the following could be the artifacts in the order of their age, from first to sixth?

(A) figurine, headdress, jar, necklace, plaque, tureen
(B) figurine, jar, plaque, headdress, tureen, necklace
(C) figurine, necklace, plaque, headdress, jar, tureen
(D) necklace, jar, figurine, headdress, plaque, tureen
(E) plaque, tureen, figurine, necklace, jar, headdress

7. Exactly how many of the artifacts are there any one of which could be first?

(A) one
(B) two
(C) three
(D) four
(E) five

8. Which one of the following artifacts CANNOT be fourth?

(A) figurine
(B) headdress
(C) jar
(D) necklace
(E) plaque

9. If the figurine is third, which one of the following must be second?

(A) headdress
(B) jar
(C) necklace
(D) plaque
(E) tureen

10. If the plaque is first, then exactly how many artifacts are there any one of which could be second?

(A) one
(B) two
(C) three
(D) four
(E) five

11. Which one of the following, if substituted for the information that the necklace and the jar are both older than the tureen, would have the same effect in determining the order of the artifacts?

(A) The tureen is older than the headdress but not as old as the figurine.
(B) The figurine and the necklace are both older than the tureen.
(C) The necklace is older than the tureen if and only if the jar is.
(D) All of the artifacts except the headdress and the plaque must be older than the tureen.
(E) The plaque is older than the necklace if and only if the plaque is older than the tureen.

GO ON TO THE NEXT PAGE.

Questions 12–17

The coach of a women's track team must determine which four of five runners—Quinn, Ramirez, Smith, Terrell, and Uzoma—will run in the four races of an upcoming track meet. Each of the four runners chosen will run in exactly one of the four races—the first, second, third, or fourth. The coach's selection is bound by the following constraints:

  If Quinn runs in the track meet, then Terrell runs in the race immediately after the race in which Quinn runs.
  Smith does not run in either the second race or the fourth race.
  If Uzoma does not run in the track meet, then Ramirez runs in the second race.
  If Ramirez runs in the second race, then Uzoma does not run in the track meet.

12. Which one of the following could be the order in which the runners run, from first to fourth?

(A) Uzoma, Ramirez, Quinn, Terrell
(B) Terrell, Smith, Ramirez, Uzoma
(C) Smith, Ramirez, Terrell, Quinn
(D) Ramirez, Uzoma, Smith, Terrell
(E) Quinn, Terrell, Smith, Ramirez

13. Which one of the following runners must the coach select to run in the track meet?

(A) Quinn
(B) Ramirez
(C) Smith
(D) Terrell
(E) Uzoma

14. The question of which runners will be chosen to run in the track meet and in what races they will run can be completely resolved if which one of the following is true?

(A) Ramirez runs in the first race.
(B) Ramirez runs in the second race.
(C) Ramirez runs in the third race.
(D) Ramirez runs in the fourth race.
(E) Ramirez does not run in the track meet.

15. Which one of the following CANNOT be true?

(A) Ramirez runs in the race immediately before the race in which Smith runs.
(B) Smith runs in the race immediately before the race in which Quinn runs.
(C) Smith runs in the race immediately before the race in which Terrell runs.
(D) Terrell runs in the race immediately before the race in which Ramirez runs.
(E) Uzoma runs in the race immediately before the race in which Terrell runs.

16. If Uzoma runs in the first race, then which one of the following must be true?

(A) Quinn does not run in the track meet.
(B) Smith does not run in the track meet.
(C) Quinn runs in the second race.
(D) Terrell runs in the second race.
(E) Ramirez runs in the fourth race.

17. If both Quinn and Smith run in the track meet, then how many of the runners are there any one of whom could be the one who runs in the first race?

(A) one
(B) two
(C) three
(D) four
(E) five

GO ON TO THE NEXT PAGE.

Questions 18–23

From the 1st through the 7th of next month, seven nurses—Farnham, Griseldi, Heany, Juarez, Khan, Lightfoot, and Moreau—will each conduct one information session at a community center. Each nurse's session will fall on a different day. The nurses' schedule is governed by the following constraints:

At least two of the other nurses' sessions must fall in between Heany's session and Moreau's session.

Griseldi's session must be on the day before Khan's.

Juarez's session must be on a later day than Moreau's.

Farnham's session must be on an earlier day than Khan's but on a later day than Lightfoot's.

Lightfoot cannot conduct the session on the 2nd.

18. Which one of the following could be the order of the nurses' sessions, from first to last?

(A) Farnham, Griseldi, Khan, Moreau, Juarez, Lightfoot, Heany

(B) Heany, Lightfoot, Farnham, Moreau, Juarez, Griseldi, Khan

(C) Juarez, Heany, Lightfoot, Farnham, Moreau, Griseldi, Khan

(D) Lightfoot, Moreau, Farnham, Juarez, Griseldi, Khan, Heany

(E) Moreau, Lightfoot, Heany, Juarez, Farnham, Griseldi, Khan

19. Juarez's session CANNOT be on which one of the following days?

(A) the 2nd
(B) the 3rd
(C) the 5th
(D) the 6th
(E) the 7th

20. If Juarez's session is on the 3rd, then which one of the following could be true?

(A) Moreau's session is on the 1st.
(B) Khan's session is on the 5th.
(C) Heany's session is on the 6th.
(D) Griseldi's session is on the 5th.
(E) Farnham's session is on the 2nd.

21. If Khan's session is on an earlier day than Moreau's, which one of the following could conduct the session on the 3rd?

(A) Griseldi
(B) Heany
(C) Juarez
(D) Lightfoot
(E) Moreau

22. If Griseldi's session is on the 5th, then which one of the following must be true?

(A) Farnham's session is on the 3rd.
(B) Heany's session is on the 7th.
(C) Juarez's session is on the 4th.
(D) Lightfoot's session is on the 1st.
(E) Moreau's session is on the 2nd.

23. Lightfoot's session could be on which one of the following days?

(A) the 3rd
(B) the 4th
(C) the 5th
(D) the 6th
(E) the 7th

S T O P

IF YOU FINISH BEFORE TIME IS CALLED, YOU MAY CHECK YOUR WORK ON THIS SECTION ONLY.
DO NOT WORK ON ANY OTHER SECTION IN THE TEST.

SECTION IV
Time—35 minutes
26 Questions

Directions: The questions in this section are based on the reasoning contained in brief statements or passages. For some questions, more than one of the choices could conceivably answer the question. However, you are to choose the best answer; that is, the response that most accurately and completely answers the question. You should not make assumptions that are by commonsense standards implausible, superfluous, or incompatible with the passage. After you have chosen the best answer, blacken the corresponding space on your answer sheet.

1. Among Trinidadian guppies, males with large spots are more attractive to females than are males with small spots, who consequently are presented with less frequent mating opportunities. Yet guppies with small spots are more likely to avoid detection by predators, so in waters where predators are abundant only guppies with small spots live to maturity.

   The situation described above most closely conforms to which one of the following generalizations?

   (A) A trait that helps attract mates is sometimes more dangerous to one sex than to another.
   (B) Those organisms that are most attractive to the opposite sex have the greatest number of offspring.
   (C) Those organisms that survive the longest have the greatest number of offspring.
   (D) Whether a trait is harmful to the organisms of a species can depend on which sex possesses it.
   (E) A trait that is helpful to procreation can also hinder it in certain environments.

2. Programmer: We computer programmers at Mytheco are demanding raises to make our average salary comparable with that of the technical writers here who receive, on average, 20 percent more in salary and benefits than we do. This pay difference is unfair and intolerable.

   Mytheco executive: But many of the technical writers have worked for Mytheco longer than have many of the programmers. Since salary and benefits at Mytheco are directly tied to seniority, the 20 percent pay difference you mention is perfectly acceptable.

   Evaluating the adequacy of the Mytheco executive's response requires a clarification of which one of the following?

   (A) whether any of the technical writers at Mytheco once worked as programmers at the company
   (B) how the average seniority of programmers compares with the average seniority of technical writers
   (C) whether the sorts of benefits an employee of Mytheco receives are tied to the salary of that employee
   (D) whether the Mytheco executive was at one time a technical writer employed by Mytheco
   (E) how the Mytheco executive's salary compares with that of the programmers

3. Cable TV stations have advantages that enable them to attract many more advertisers than broadcast networks attract. For example, cable stations are able to target particular audiences with 24-hour news, sports, or movies, whereas broadcast networks must offer a variety of programming. Cable can also offer lower advertising rates than any broadcast network can, because it is subsidized by viewers through subscriber fees. Additionally, many cable stations have expanded worldwide with multinational programming.

   The statements above, if true, provide support for each of the following EXCEPT:

   (A) Some broadcast networks can be viewed in several countries.
   (B) Broadcast networks do not rely on subscriber fees from viewers.
   (C) Low costs are often an important factor for advertisers in selecting a station or network on which to run a TV ad.
   (D) Some advertisers prefer to have the opportunity to address a worldwide audience.
   (E) The audiences that some advertisers prefer to target watch 24-hour news stations.

4. In polluted industrial English cities during the Industrial Revolution, two plant diseases—black spot, which infects roses, and tar spot, which infects sycamore trees—disappeared. It is likely that air pollution eradicated these diseases.

   Which one of the following, if true, most strengthens the reasoning above?

   (A) Scientists theorize that some plants can develop a resistance to air pollution.
   (B) Certain measures help prevent infection by black spot and tar spot, but once infection occurs, it is very difficult to eliminate.
   (C) For many plant species, scientists have not determined the effects of air pollution.
   (D) Black spot and tar spot returned when the air in the cities became less polluted.
   (E) Black spot and tar spot were the only plant diseases that disappeared in any English cities during the Industrial Revolution.

GO ON TO THE NEXT PAGE.

5. Many scholars are puzzled about who created the seventeenth-century abridgment of Shakespeare's *Hamlet* contained in the First Quarto. Two facts about the work shed light on this question. First, the person who undertook the abridgment clearly did not possess a copy of *Hamlet*. Second, the abridgment contains a very accurate rendering of the speeches of one of the characters, but a slipshod handling of all the other parts.

Which one of the following statements is most supported by the information above?

(A) The abridgment was prepared by Shakespeare.
(B) The abridgment was created to make *Hamlet* easier to produce on stage.
(C) The abridgment was produced by an actor who had played a role in *Hamlet*.
(D) The abridgement was prepared by a spectator of a performance of *Hamlet*.
(E) The abridgment was produced by an actor who was trying to improve the play.

6. Musicologist: Many critics complain of the disproportion between text and music in Handel's *da capo* arias. These texts are generally quite short and often repeated well beyond what is needed for literal understanding. Yet such criticism is refuted by noting that repetition serves a vital function: it frees the audience to focus on the music itself, which can speak to audiences whatever their language.

Which one of the following sentences best expresses the main point of the musicologist's reasoning?

(A) Handel's *da capo* arias contain a disproportionate amount of music.
(B) Handel's *da capo* arias are superior to most in their accessibility to diverse audiences.
(C) At least one frequent criticism of Handel's *da capo* arias is undeserved.
(D) At least some of Handel's *da capo* arias contain unnecessary repetitions.
(E) Most criticism of Handel's *da capo* arias is unwarranted.

7. Baxe Interiors, one of the largest interior design companies in existence, currently has a near monopoly in the corporate market. Several small design companies have won prestigious awards for their corporate work, while Baxe has won none. Nonetheless, the corporate managers who solicit design proposals will only contract with companies they believe are unlikely to go bankrupt, and they believe that only very large companies are unlikely to go bankrupt.

The statements above, if true, most strongly support which one of the following?

(A) There are other very large design companies besides Baxe, but they produce designs that are inferior to Baxe's.
(B) Baxe does not have a near monopoly in the market of any category of interior design other than corporate interiors.
(C) For the most part, designs that are produced by small companies are superior to the designs produced by Baxe.
(D) At least some of the corporate managers who solicit design proposals are unaware that there are designs that are much better than those produced by Baxe.
(E) The existence of interior designs that are superior to those produced by Baxe does not currently threaten its near monopoly in the corporate market.

GO ON TO THE NEXT PAGE.

8. The giant Chicxulub crater in Mexico provides indisputable evidence that a huge asteroid, about six miles across, struck Earth around the time many of the last dinosaur species were becoming extinct. But this catastrophe was probably not responsible for most of these extinctions. Any major asteroid strike kills many organisms in or near the region of the impact, but there is little evidence that such a strike could have a worldwide effect. Indeed, some craters even larger than the Chicxulub crater were made during times in Earth's history when there were no known extinctions.

Which one of the following, if true, would most weaken the argument?

(A) The vast majority of dinosaur species are known to have gone extinct well before the time of the asteroid impact that produced the Chicxulub crater.

(B) The size of a crater caused by an asteroid striking Earth generally depends on both the size of that asteroid and the force of its impact.

(C) Fossils have been discovered of a number of dinosaurs that clearly died as a result of the asteroid impact that produced the Chicxulub crater.

(D) There is no evidence that any other asteroid of equal size struck Earth at the same time as the asteroid that produced the Chicxulub crater.

(E) During the period immediately before the asteroid that produced the Chicxulub crater struck, most of the world's dinosaurs lived in or near the region of the asteroid's impending impact.

9. In a sample containing 1,000 peanuts from lot A and 1,000 peanuts from lot B, 50 of the peanuts from lot A were found to be infected with *Aspergillus*. Two hundred of the peanuts from lot B were found to be infected with *Aspergillus*. Therefore, infection with *Aspergillus* is more widespread in lot B than in lot A.

The reasoning in which one of the following is most similar to the reasoning in the argument above?

(A) Every one of these varied machine parts is of uniformly high quality. Therefore, the machine that we assemble from them will be of equally high quality.

(B) If a plant is carelessly treated, it is likely to develop blight. If a plant develops blight, it is likely to die. Therefore, if a plant is carelessly treated, it is likely to die.

(C) In the past 1,000 experiments, whenever an experimental fungicide was applied to coffee plants infected with coffee rust, the infection disappeared. The coffee rust never disappeared before the fungicide was applied. Therefore, in these experiments, application of the fungicide caused the disappearance of coffee rust.

(D) Three thousand registered voters—1,500 members of the Liberal party and 1,500 members of the Conservative party—were asked which mayoral candidate they favored. Four hundred of the Liberals and 300 of the Conservatives favored Pollack. Therefore, Pollack has more support among Liberals than among Conservatives.

(E) All of my livestock are registered with the regional authority. None of the livestock registered with the regional authority are free-range livestock. Therefore, none of my livestock are free-range livestock.

GO ON TO THE NEXT PAGE.

10. Economist: If the belief were to become widespread that losing one's job is not a sign of personal shortcomings but instead an effect of impersonal social forces (which is surely correct), there would be growth in the societal demand for more government control of the economy to protect individuals from these forces, just as the government now protects them from military invasion. Such extensive government control of the economy would lead to an economic disaster, however.

The economist's statements, if true, most strongly support which one of the following?

(A) Increased knowledge of the causes of job loss could lead to economic disaster.

(B) An individual's belief in his or her own abilities is the only reliable protection against impersonal social forces.

(C) Governments should never interfere with economic forces.

(D) Societal demand for government control of the economy is growing.

(E) In general, people should feel no more responsible for economic disasters than for military invasions.

11. A development company has proposed building an airport near the city of Dalton. If the majority of Dalton's residents favor the proposal, the airport will be built. However, it is unlikely that a majority of Dalton's residents would favor the proposal, for most of them believe that the airport would create noise problems. Thus, it is unlikely that the airport will be built.

The reasoning in the argument is flawed in that the argument

(A) treats a sufficient condition for the airport's being built as a necessary condition

(B) concludes that something must be true, because most people believe it to be true

(C) concludes, on the basis that a certain event is unlikely to occur, that the event will not occur

(D) fails to consider whether people living near Dalton would favor building the airport

(E) overlooks the possibility that a new airport could benefit the local economy

12. After the rush-hour speed limit on the British M25 motorway was lowered from 70 miles per hour (115 kilometers per hour) to 50 miles per hour (80 kilometers per hour), rush-hour travel times decreased by approximately 15 percent.

Which one of the following, if true, most helps to explain the decrease in travel times described above?

(A) After the decrease in the rush-hour speed limit, the average speed on the M25 was significantly lower during rush hours than at other times of the day.

(B) Travel times during periods other than rush hours were essentially unchanged after the rush-hour speed limit was lowered.

(C) Before the rush-hour speed limit was lowered, rush-hour accidents that caused lengthy delays were common, and most of these accidents were caused by high-speed driving.

(D) Enforcement of speed limits on the M25 was quite rigorous both before and after the rush-hour speed limit was lowered.

(E) The number of people who drive on the M25 during rush hours did not increase after the rush-hour speed limit was lowered.

13. An art critic, by ridiculing an artwork, can undermine the pleasure one takes in it; conversely, by lavishing praise upon an artwork, an art critic can render the experience of viewing the artwork more pleasurable. So an artwork's artistic merit can depend not only on the person who creates it but also on those who critically evaluate it.

The conclusion can be properly drawn if which one of the following is assumed?

(A) The merit of an artistic work is determined by the amount of pleasure it elicits.

(B) Most people lack the confidence necessary for making their own evaluations of art.

(C) Art critics understand what gives an artwork artistic merit better than artists do.

(D) Most people seek out critical reviews of particular artworks before viewing those works.

(E) The pleasure people take in something is typically influenced by what they think others feel about it.

GO ON TO THE NEXT PAGE.

14. The number of automobile thefts has declined steadily during the past five years, and it is more likely now than it was five years ago that someone who steals a car will be convicted of the crime.

Which one of the following, if true, most helps to explain the facts cited above?

(A) Although there are fewer car thieves now than there were five years ago, the proportion of thieves who tend to abandon cars before their owners notice that they have been stolen has also decreased.

(B) Car alarms are more common than they were five years ago, but their propensity to be triggered in the absence of any criminal activity has resulted in people generally ignoring them when they are triggered.

(C) An upsurge in home burglaries over the last five years has required police departments to divert limited resources to investigation of these cases.

(D) Because of the increasingly lucrative market for stolen automobile parts, many stolen cars are quickly disassembled and the parts are sold to various buyers across the country.

(E) There are more adolescent car thieves now than there were five years ago, and the sentences given to young criminals tend to be far more lenient than those given to adult criminals.

15. Legislator: My staff conducted a poll in which my constituents were asked whether they favor high taxes. More than 97 percent answered "no." Clearly, then, my constituents would support the bill I recently introduced, which reduces the corporate income tax.

The reasoning in the legislator's argument is most vulnerable to criticism on the grounds that the argument

(A) fails to establish that the opinions of the legislator's constituents are representative of the opinions of the country's population as a whole

(B) fails to consider whether the legislator's constituents consider the current corporate income tax a high tax

(C) confuses an absence of evidence that the legislator's constituents oppose a bill with the existence of evidence that the legislator's constituents support that bill

(D) draws a conclusion that merely restates a claim presented in support of that conclusion

(E) treats a result that proves that the public supports a bill as a result that is merely consistent with public support for that bill

16. Many nursing homes have prohibitions against having pets, and these should be lifted. The presence of an animal companion can yield health benefits by reducing a person's stress. A pet can also make one's time at a home more rewarding, which will be important to more people as the average life span of our population increases.

Which one of the following most accurately expresses the conclusion drawn in the argument above?

(A) As the average life span increases, it will be important to more people that life in nursing homes be rewarding.

(B) Residents of nursing homes should enjoy the same rewarding aspects of life as anyone else.

(C) The policy that many nursing homes have should be changed so that residents are allowed to have pets.

(D) Having a pet can reduce one's stress and thereby make one a healthier person.

(E) The benefits older people derive from having pets need to be recognized, especially as the average life span increases.

17. Near many cities, contamination of lakes and rivers from pollutants in rainwater runoff exceeds that from industrial discharge. As the runoff washes over buildings and pavements, it picks up oil and other pollutants. Thus, water itself is among the biggest water polluters.

The statement that contamination of lakes and rivers from pollutants in rainwater runoff exceeds that from industrial discharge plays which one of the following roles in the argument?

(A) It is a conclusion for which the claim that water itself should be considered a polluter is offered as support.

(B) It is cited as evidence that pollution from rainwater runoff is a more serious problem than pollution from industrial discharge.

(C) It is a generalization based on the observation that rainwater runoff picks up oil and other pollutants as it washes over buildings and pavements.

(D) It is a premise offered in support of the conclusion that water itself is among the biggest water polluters.

(E) It is stated to provide an example of a typical kind of city pollution.

GO ON TO THE NEXT PAGE.

18. Wong: Although all countries are better off as democracies, a transitional autocratic stage is sometimes required before a country can become democratic.

Tate: The freedom and autonomy that democracy provides are of genuine value, but the simple material needs of people are more important. Some countries can better meet these needs as autocracies than as democracies.

Wong's and Tate's statements provide the most support for the claim that they disagree over the truth of which one of the following?

(A) There are some countries that are better off as autocracies than as democracies.
(B) Nothing is more important to a country than the freedom and autonomy of the individuals who live in that country.
(C) In some cases, a country cannot become a democracy.
(D) The freedom and autonomy that democracy provides are of genuine value.
(E) All democracies succeed in meeting the simple material needs of people.

19. Principle: When none of the fully qualified candidates for a new position at Arvue Corporation currently works for that company, it should hire the candidate who would be most productive in that position.

Application: Arvue should not hire Krall for the new position, because Delacruz is a candidate and is fully qualified.

Which one of the following, if true, justifies the above application of the principle?

(A) All of the candidates are fully qualified for the new position, but none already works for Arvue.
(B) Of all the candidates who do not already work for Arvue, Delacruz would be the most productive in the new position.
(C) Krall works for Arvue, but Delacruz is the candidate who would be most productive in the new position.
(D) Several candidates currently work for Arvue, but Krall and Delacruz do not.
(E) None of the candidates already works for Arvue, and Delacruz is the candidate who would be most productive in the new position.

20. Many important types of medicine have been developed from substances discovered in plants that grow only in tropical rain forests. There are thousands of plant species in these rain forests that have not yet been studied by scientists, and it is very likely that many such plants also contain substances of medicinal value. Thus, if the tropical rain forests are not preserved, important types of medicine will never be developed.

Which one of the following is an assumption required by the argument?

(A) There are substances of medicinal value contained in tropical rain forest plants not yet studied by scientists that differ from those substances already discovered in tropical rain forest plants.
(B) Most of the tropical rain forest plants that contain substances of medicinal value can also be found growing in other types of environment.
(C) The majority of plant species that are unique to tropical rain forests and that have been studied by scientists have been discovered to contain substances of medicinal value.
(D) Any substance of medicinal value contained in plant species indigenous to tropical rain forests will eventually be discovered if those species are studied by scientists.
(E) The tropical rain forests should be preserved to make it possible for important medicines to be developed from plant species that have not yet been studied by scientists.

GO ON TO THE NEXT PAGE.

21. In modern deep-diving marine mammals, such as whales, the outer shell of the bones is porous. This has the effect of making the bones light enough so that it is easy for the animals to swim back to the surface after a deep dive. The outer shell of the bones was also porous in the ichthyosaur, an extinct prehistoric marine reptile. We can conclude from this that ichthyosaurs were deep divers.

Which one of the following, if true, most weakens the argument?

(A) Some deep-diving marine species must surface after dives but do not have bones with porous outer shells.

(B) In most modern marine reptile species, the outer shell of the bones is not porous.

(C) In most modern and prehistoric marine reptile species that are not deep divers, the outer shell of the bones is porous.

(D) In addition to the porous outer shells of their bones, whales have at least some characteristics suited to deep diving for which there is no clear evidence whether these were shared by ichthyosaurs.

(E) There is evidence that the bones of ichthyosaurs would have been light enough to allow surfacing even if the outer shells were not porous.

22. Librarian: Some argue that the preservation grant we received should be used to restore our original copy of our town's charter, since if the charter is not restored, it will soon deteriorate beyond repair. But this document, although sentimentally important, has no scholarly value. Copies are readily available. Since we are a research library and not a museum, the money would be better spent preserving documents that have significant scholarly value.

The claim that the town's charter, if not restored, will soon deteriorate beyond repair plays which one of the following roles in the librarian's argument?

(A) It is a claim that the librarian's argument attempts to show to be false.

(B) It is the conclusion of the argument that the librarian's argument rejects.

(C) It is a premise in an argument whose conclusion is rejected by the librarian's argument.

(D) It is a premise used to support the librarian's main conclusion.

(E) It is a claim whose truth is required by the librarian's argument.

23. Columnist: Although much has been learned, we are still largely ignorant of the intricate interrelationships among species of living organisms. We should, therefore, try to preserve the maximum number of species if we have an interest in preserving any, since allowing species toward which we are indifferent to perish might undermine the viability of other species.

Which one of the following principles, if valid, most helps to justify the columnist's argument?

(A) It is strongly in our interest to preserve certain plant and animal species.

(B) We should not take any action until all relevant scientific facts have been established and taken into account.

(C) We should not allow the number of species to diminish any further than is necessary for the flourishing of present and future human populations.

(D) We should not allow a change to occur unless we are assured that that change will not jeopardize anything that is important to us.

(E) We should always undertake the course of action that is likely to have the best consequences in the immediate future.

24. One is likely to feel comfortable approaching a stranger if the stranger is of one's approximate age. Therefore, long-term friends are probably of the same approximate age as each other since most long-term friendships begin because someone felt comfortable approaching a stranger.

The reasoning in the argument is flawed in that it

(A) presumes, without warrant, that one is likely to feel uncomfortable approaching a person only if that person is a stranger

(B) infers that a characteristic is present in a situation from the fact that that characteristic is present in most similar situations

(C) overlooks the possibility that one is less likely to feel comfortable approaching someone who is one's approximate age if that person is a stranger than if that person is not a stranger

(D) presumes, without warrant, that one never approaches a stranger unless one feels comfortable doing so

(E) fails to address whether one is likely to feel comfortable approaching a stranger who is not one's approximate age

GO ON TO THE NEXT PAGE.

25. There can be no individual freedom without the rule of law, for there is no individual freedom without social integrity, and pursuing the good life is not possible without social integrity.

The conclusion drawn above follows logically if which one of the following is assumed?

(A)   There can be no rule of law without social integrity.
(B)   There can be no social integrity without the rule of law.
(C)   One cannot pursue the good life without the rule of law.
(D)   Social integrity is possible only if individual freedom prevails.
(E)   There can be no rule of law without individual freedom.

26. Economist: Countries with an uneducated population are destined to be weak economically and politically, whereas those with an educated population have governments that display a serious financial commitment to public education. So any nation with a government that has made such a commitment will avoid economic and political weakness.

The pattern of flawed reasoning in which one of the following arguments is most similar to that in the economist's argument?

(A)   Animal species with a very narrow diet will have more difficulty surviving if the climate suddenly changes, but a species with a broader diet will not; for changes in the climate can remove the traditional food supply.
(B)   People incapable of empathy are not good candidates for public office, but those who do have the capacity for empathy are able to manipulate others easily; hence, people who can manipulate others are good candidates for public office.
(C)   People who cannot give orders are those who do not understand the personalities of the people to whom they give orders. Thus, those who can give orders are those who understand the personalities of the people to whom they give orders.
(D)   Poets who create poetry of high quality are those who have studied traditional poetry, because poets who have not studied traditional poetry are the poets most likely to create something shockingly inventive, and poetry that is shockingly inventive is rarely fine poetry.
(E)   People who dislike exercise are unlikely to lose weight without sharply curtailing their food intake; but since those who dislike activity generally tend to avoid it, people who like to eat but dislike exercise will probably fail to lose weight.

S T O P
IF YOU FINISH BEFORE TIME IS CALLED, YOU MAY CHECK YOUR WORK ON THIS SECTION ONLY.
DO NOT WORK ON ANY OTHER SECTION IN THE TEST.

COMPUTING YOUR SCORE

Directions:

1. Use the Answer Key on the next page to check your answers.

2. Use the Scoring Worksheet below to compute your raw score.

3. Use the Score Conversion Chart to convert your raw score into the 120–180 scale.

Scoring Worksheet

1. Enter the number of questions you answered correctly in each section.

	Number Correct
SECTION I..................	_____
SECTION II..................	_____
SECTION III..............	_____
SECTION IV	_____

2. Enter the sum here: _____
   This is your Raw Score.

Conversion Chart
For Converting Raw Score to the 120–180 LSAT Scaled Score
LSAT Form 0LSN86

Reported Score	Raw Score Lowest	Raw Score Highest
180	99	101
179	98	98
178	97	97
177	96	96
176	—*	—*
175	95	95
174	94	94
173	93	93
172	92	92
171	91	91
170	89	90
169	88	88
168	87	87
167	85	86
166	84	84
165	82	83
164	81	81
163	79	80
162	78	78
161	76	77
160	74	75
159	73	73
158	71	72
157	69	70
156	67	68
155	66	66
154	64	65
153	62	63
152	60	61
151	58	59
150	57	57
149	55	56
148	53	54
147	52	52
146	50	51
145	48	49
144	47	47
143	45	46
142	43	44
141	42	42
140	40	41
139	39	39
138	37	38
137	36	36
136	34	35
135	33	33
134	31	32
133	30	30
132	29	29
131	27	28
130	26	26
129	25	25
128	24	24
127	22	23
126	21	21
125	20	20
124	19	19
123	18	18
122	16	17
121	—*	—*
120	0	15

*There is no raw score that will produce this scaled score for this form.

ANSWER KEY

SECTION I

1.	D	8.	A	15.	A	22.	A
2.	B	9.	E	16.	D	23.	E
3.	B	10.	C	17.	D	24.	E
4.	D	11.	B	18.	C	25.	B
5.	E	12.	E	19.	B	26.	A
6.	A	13.	B	20.	D	27.	B
7.	C	14.	B	21.	E		

SECTION II

1.	D	8.	A	15.	B	22.	C
2.	E	9.	E	16.	C	23.	D
3.	C	10.	A	17.	A	24.	B
4.	D	11.	A	18.	A	25.	D
5.	A	12.	A	19.	D		
6.	C	13.	B	20.	C		
7.	D	14.	D	21.	E		

SECTION III

1.	A	8.	A	15.	A	22.	B
2.	E	9.	C	16.	E	23.	A
3.	A	10.	B	17.	B		
4.	C	11.	D	18.	D		
5.	D	12.	D	19.	C		
6.	A	13.	D	20.	D		
7.	C	14.	B	21.	B		

SECTION IV

1.	E	8.	E	15.	B	22.	C
2.	B	9.	D	16.	C	23.	D
3.	A	10.	A	17.	D	24.	E
4.	D	11.	A	18.	A	25.	B
5.	C	12.	C	19.	E	26.	B
6.	C	13.	A	20.	A		
7.	E	14.	A	21.	C		

SECTION
ONE

Reading Comprehension

(Or: Fake It 'Til You Make It)

The key to the Reading Comprehension section of the LSAT is to accept, in advance, that the passages are probably going to be boring as hell.

If I were reading any of these passages in a magazine, I'd probably skip to the next story. Unfortunately, that's not an option on the LSAT. It's critical that we 1) stay awake, and 2) understand as much as possible about the passage from *one* read-through. The absolute enemy here is that sort of "reading" where our eyes glaze over and we spend five minutes looking at the words, only to realize that we haven't the foggiest idea what the passage actually says.

In order to stay as present as possible, I use a little device I call *Why are you wasting my time with this?* It's a very simple concept with powerful results. I pretend that the author of any given passage has stopped me on the street and is telling me a long, rambling, boring story. I just want to pick up my Chinese takeout, so I'm impatiently trying to make them get to the point. I ask the author, repeatedly: *Why are you wasting my time with this?*

For me, taking this nasty attitude helps me focus on what the author is saying. I may not get every single detail; in fact, I'm necessarily tuning out some of the noise in order to find the main point. I know that the author is going to say in 60 lines what he could have said in 10. By asking the author why he's wasting my time after every paragraph, I'm able to home in on the author's main thesis and attitude. I'm also able to stay awake. The good news is, if we fake interest for a while, we might find ourselves actually getting interested. Fake it 'til you make it.

Let's dig in...

Passage One (Questions 1-6)

The Universal Declaration of Human Rights (UDHR), approved by the United Nations General Assembly in 1948, was the first international treaty to expressly affirm universal respect for human rights.

(5) Prior to 1948 no truly international standard of humanitarian beliefs existed. Although Article 1 of the 1945 UN Charter had been written with the express purpose of obligating the UN to "encourage respect for human rights and for fundamental

(10) freedoms for all without distinction as to race, sex, language, or religion," there were members of delegations from various small countries and representatives of several nongovernmental organizations who felt that the language of Article 1

(15) was not strong enough, and that the Charter as a whole did not go far enough in its efforts to guarantee basic human rights. This group lobbied vigorously to strengthen the Charter's human rights provisions and proposed that member states be

(20) required "to take separate and joint action and to co-operate with the organization for the promotion of human rights." This would have implied an obligation for member states to act on human rights issues. Ultimately, this proposal and others like it were not

(25) adopted; instead, the UDHR was commissioned and drafted.

The original mandate for producing the document was given to the UN Commission on Human Rights in February 1946. Between that time and the General

(30) Assembly's final approval of the document, the UDHR passed through an elaborate eight-stage drafting process in which it made its way through almost every level of the UN hierarchy. The articles were debated at each stage, and all 30 articles were

(35) argued passionately by delegates representing diverse ideologies, traditions, and cultures. The document as it was finally approved set forth the essential principles of freedom and equality for everyone—regardless of sex, race, color, language, religion,

(40) political or other opinion, national or social origin, property, birth or other status. It also asserted a number of fundamental human rights, including among others the right to work, the right to rest and leisure, and the right to education.

(45) While the UDHR is in many ways a progressive document, it also has weaknesses, the most regrettable of which is its nonbinding legal status. For all its strong language and high ideals, the UDHR remains a resolution of a purely programmatic nature.

(50) Nevertheless, the document has led, even if belatedly, to the creation of legally binding human rights conventions, and it clearly deserves recognition as an international standard-setting piece of work, as a set of aspirations to which UN member states are

(55) intended to strive, and as a call to arms in the name of humanity, justice, and freedom.

This was an easier-than-average passage because the author's attitude was present right from the get-go. There's no doubt that the author is in favor of human rights. (We're very unlikely to read a passage on the LSAT that would argue against human rights.) Furthermore, the author specifically thinks that the Universal Declaration of Human Rights is a good thing. She says the UDHR was the "first" to expressly affirm human rights, and that prior to the UDHR, there was no "truly international standard." It's very likely that she's here to tell us that the UDHR is a good thing.

At the end of the first paragraph, we ask *Why are you wasting my time with this?* The author would respond with something like "The UDHR is good because it was the first truly international standard."

The beginning of the second paragraph provides details about the adoption process of the UDHR, and the end of the second paragraph provides details about what's contained in the UDHR. None of this changes the main point of the passage, and I'm not terribly concerned about these details when I read them. (Remember, we know in advance that this passage is going to be terribly written. We're trying to somehow turn 60 lines of bullshit into 10 lines of gold. Don't get distracted from the main point.) We'll probably have to refer back to this paragraph when one of the questions asks us to remember some details, but don't make an extraordinary effort to remember them as you go. They'll be there, in the second paragraph, if we need them.

The last paragraph mentions weaknesses of the UDHR, primarily its nonbinding legal status. The last paragraph closes by stating that the UDHR led to legally binding conventions, even if it wasn't binding itself, and says it "clearly deserves recognition."

So: *Why are you wasting my time with this?* The main point of the entire passage is something like "The UDHR, while nonbinding, was the first truly international standard for human rights, led to the eventual adoption of legally binding conventions, and is therefore worthy of recognition." If you're able to get that much out of the passage, you've won half the battle.

Hackers swing much harder than professional golfers do. Beer league bowlers roll the ball much faster than professional bowlers do. And the average LSAT student, believe it or not, reads through the passage faster than I do. The difference is that I read it *once*. Take your time through the passage, make *sure* you've got the main point, and you'll crush the questions, even if you have to make quick trips back to the passage for the occasional detail. If you don't have the main point before you proceed to the questions, you're doing it wrong. Once you get to the questions, remember that the main point should color your answer to every question.

QUESTION 1:

By referring to the Universal Declaration of Human Rights as "purely programmatic" (line 49) in nature, the author most likely intends to emphasize

A) the likelihood that the document will inspire innovative government programs designed to safeguard human rights
B) the ability of the document's drafters to translate abstract ideals into concrete standards
C) the compromises that went into producing a version of the document that would garner the approval of all relevant parties
D) the fact that the guidelines established by the document are ultimately unenforceable
E) the frustration experienced by the document's drafters at stubborn resistance from within the UN hierarchy

This question asks about the use of a specific phrase, "purely programmatic," in line 49. I didn't know what this meant as I read through the passage. (If something in the passage seems foreign to you, it's a good bet that there will be a question about it.) Context is very important here. The point of the beginning of the third paragraph—as noted above—is that the UDHR is nonbinding. So we can sensibly guess that "purely programmatic" must mean nonbinding in this context—totally reasonable. Hopefully we'll find that in the answer choices.

A) "Innovative" doesn't mean nonbinding.
B) "Abstract" doesn't mean nonbinding.
C) "Compromises" doesn't mean nonbinding.
D) "Unenforceable" is very close to nonbinding, so this is our answer. But we're going to read all five, just in case this is some kind of trap.
E) "Stubborn resistance" has nothing to do with nonbinding. Our answer is D.

2

QUESTION 2:

The author most probably quotes directly from both the UN Charter (lines 8–11) and the proposal mentioned in lines 20–22 for which one of the following reasons?

A) to contrast the different definitions of human rights in the two documents
B) to compare the strength of the human rights language in the two documents
C) to identify a bureaucratic vocabulary that is common to the two documents
D) to highlight what the author believes to be the most important point in each document
E) to call attention to a significant difference in the prose styles of the two documents

This question asks about two quotes from the passage. Remember these off the top of your head? Me neither. Let's return to the passage to for a quick detail run. In order to get context, you usually have to read more than just the lines that are cited. Get in the habit of going back a few lines earlier to get the big picture. Taken together, lines 5–22 are about a failed proposal to give teeth to the human rights language in the UN Charter. The first citation (lines 8–11) is the relatively weak suggestion that member nations "encourage respect for human rights," and the second citation (lines 20–22) is the failed, stronger language that would have obligated member nations "to take action" to enforce human rights. The author is comparing the actual Charter to the failed, stronger amendment.

A) The lines cited don't exactly define human rights, so I don't think this can be the answer.
B) This matches my advance answer, so that's the frontrunner thus far.
C) We already decided that the author isn't wasting our time with an analysis of "bureaucratic vocabulary." The author's primary concern is human rights.
D) The language cited in lines 8–11 is not presented as "the main point" of the UN Charter. This can't be the answer.
E) The author isn't wasting our time with a discussion of the prose styles of the two documents. The author is concerned with human rights. Our answer is B.

3

QUESTION 3:

The author's stance toward the Universal Declaration of Human Rights can best be described as

A) unbridled enthusiasm
B) qualified approval
C) absolute neutrality
D) reluctant rejection
E) strong hostility

These questions are very easy if you're reading the passage with the proper focus on the author's main point and attitude. How does the author feel about the UDHR? My advance answer is simply: "The author likes it."

A) The author's enthusiasm for the UDHR is not "unbridled," because of the thoughtful criticism offered in the third paragraph.
B) The author certainly approves of the UDHR, and "qualifies" his or her approval in the third paragraph by mentioning the fact that it was nonbinding. This looks good.
C) The author is definitely not neutral toward the UDHR.
D) The author certainly doesn't reject the UDHR.
E) The author is absolutely not hostile toward the UDHR. Our answer is B.

QUESTION 4:

According to the passage, each of the following is true of the Universal Declaration of Human Rights EXCEPT:

A) It asserts a right to rest and leisure.
B) It was drafted after the UN Charter was drafted.
C) The UN Commission on Human Rights was charged with producing it.
D) It has had no practical consequences.
E) It was the first international treaty to explicitly affirm universal respect for human rights.

The phrasing "according to the passage, each is true EXCEPT" requires us to refer back to the passage to eliminate truths about the UDHR that were specifically discussed. So at the end, we'll be left with the correct answer, which won't be found anywhere in the passage (or which will be specifically untrue according to the passage.)

A) The UDHR provides for a right to "rest and leisure" according to lines 43–44 of the passage.
B) The first paragraph says the UN Charter was written in 1945, and the beginning of the second paragraph says the creation of the UDHR wasn't mandated until 1946, so this is true.
C) Lines 27–28 say the UDHR was produced by the UN Commission on Human Rights.
D) The third paragraph talks about the eventual adoption of legally binding human rights conventions that sprung from the UDHR. This constitutes a practical consequence, so it cannot be true that there are "no practical consequences." This is probably the correct answer.
E) The first paragraph says the UDHR was indeed the first international treaty to explicitly affirm universal respect for human rights. Our answer is D.

> ## Dealing with "Except"
>
> When you see "EXCEPT," focus on the difference between the right and wrong answers. If the four incorrect answers "must be true," then the one correct answer COULD be false. Here, the four incorrect answers "must be true," so the single correct answer could be false.

QUESTION 5:

The author would be most likely to agree with which one of the following statements?

A) The human rights language contained in Article 1 of the UN Charter is so ambiguous as to be almost wholly ineffectual.

B) The weaknesses of the Universal Declaration of Human Rights generally outweigh the strengths of the document.

C) It was relatively easy for the drafters of the Universal Declaration of Human Rights to reach a consensus concerning the contents of the document.

D) The drafters of the Universal Declaration of Human Rights omitted important rights that should be included in a truly comprehensive list of basic human rights.

E) The Universal Declaration of Human Rights would be truer to the intentions of its staunchest proponents if UN member countries were required by law to abide by its provisions.

The only way to answer this question is to go through the answer choices one by one. It is critical to remember the author's main point while doing so. As we head into the answer choices, I'm thinking "The UDHR, while nonbinding, was nonetheless groundbreaking and influential as an international standard for human rights."

A) The language of this answer choice is too strong for my taste. Has the author really put himself in a position of calling the original UN Charter "wholly ineffectual" on human rights? Doubtful.

B) The author acknowledges the imperfections of the UDHR, but is certainly in favor of the UDHR as a whole. This can't be the answer.

C) The details are hazy, but I do remember that the process of writing the UDHR seemed to be an arduous one (beginning of paragraph two). The author definitely didn't make it sound "easy."

D) No document is perfect, and it is almost certainly true that the UDHR didn't account for every basic human right. (I didn't see a provision for sexuality, for example.) However, the author never mentioned any such holes in the UDHR, so this can't be the answer.

E) This answer choice seemed, at first, to be too negative toward the UDHR. But it is true that the "staunchest proponents" of the UDHR would want it to be binding. Since none of the other answer choices is any good, this is our answer.

QUESTION 6:

Suppose that a group of independent journalists has uncovered evidence of human rights abuses being perpetrated by a security agency of a UN member state upon a group of political dissidents. Which one of the following approaches to the situation would most likely be advocated by present-day delegates who share the views of the delegates and representatives mentioned in lines 11–14?

A) The UN General Assembly authenticates the evidence and then insists upon prompt remedial action on the part of the government of the member state.
B) The UN General Assembly stipulates that any proposed response must be unanimously accepted by member states before it can be implemented.
C) The UN issues a report critical of the actions of the member state in question and calls for a censure vote in the General Assembly.
D) The situation is regarded by the UN as an internal matter that is best left to the discretion of the government of the member state.
E) The situation is investigated further by nongovernmental humanitarian organizations that promise to disclose their findings to the public via the international media.

The delegates and representatives mentioned in lines 11–14 were in favor of a binding human-rights convention. So present-day delegates who share these beliefs would probably react quite negatively to a UN member state that was abusing the human rights of political dissidents. Their desired response would likely include prompt and stiff sanctions against the country by other UN member states. This will be our advance answer.

A) I like this answer. It seems reasonable that the UN General Assembly would need to first make sure that the violations were, indeed, occurring. Once this was accomplished, the General Assembly would "insist" upon "prompt" action. This seems appropriately stern.
B) Bureaucratic gridlock is exactly what the human rights proponents would *not* want.
C) A "report" and a "censure vote" are purely programmatic (as the author would say), and therefore aren't strong enough.
D) The human rights proponents would definitely not want to leave anything to the "discretion" of the abusing state.
E) The human rights proponents would insist on action from the UN. Leaving it to the NGOs would not be enough. The best answer is A.

Passage Two (Questions 7-13)

It is commonly assumed that even if some forgeries have aesthetic merit, no forgery has as much as an original by the imitated artist would. Yet even the most prominent art specialists can be duped by a
(5) talented artist turned forger into mistaking an almost perfect forgery for an original. For instance, artist Han van Meegeren's *The Disciples at Emmaus* (1937)—painted under the forged signature of the acclaimed Dutch master Jan Vermeer (1632-1675)—
(10) attracted lavish praise from experts as one of Vermeer's finest works. The painting hung in a Rotterdam museum until 1945, when, to the great embarrassment of the critics, van Meegeren revealed its origin. Astonishingly, there was at least one highly
(15) reputed critic who persisted in believing it to be a Vermeer even after van Meegeren's confession.

Given the experts' initial enthusiasm, some philosophers argue that van Meegeren's painting must have possessed aesthetic characteristics that, in a
(20) Vermeer original, would have justified the critics' plaudits. Van Meegeren's *Emmaus* thus raises difficult questions regarding the status of superbly executed forgeries. Is a forgery inherently inferior as art? How are we justified, if indeed we are, in revising
(25) downwards our critical assessment of a work unmasked as a forgery? Philosopher of art Alfred Lessing proposes convincing answers to these questions.

A forged work is indeed inferior as art, Lessing
(30) argues, but not because of a shortfall in aesthetic

qualities strictly defined, that is to say, in the qualities perceptible on the picture's surface. For example, in its composition, its technique, and its brilliant use of color, van Meegeren's work is flawless, even
(35) beautiful. Lessing argues instead that the deficiency lies in what might be called the painting's intangible qualities. All art, explains Lessing, involves technique, but not all art involves origination of a new vision, and originality of vision is one of the
(40) fundamental qualities by which artistic, as opposed to purely aesthetic, accomplishment is measured. Thus Vermeer is acclaimed for having inaugurated, in the seventeenth century, a new way of seeing, and for pioneering techniques for embodying this new way of
(45) seeing through distinctive treatment of light, color, and form.

Even if we grant that van Meegeren, with his undoubted mastery of Vermeer's innovative techniques, produced an aesthetically superior
(50) painting, he did so about three centuries after Vermeer developed the techniques in question. Whereas Vermeer's origination of these techniques in the seventeenth century represents a truly impressive and historic achievement, van Meegeren's production
(55) of *The Disciples at Emmaus* in the twentieth century presents nothing new or creative to the history of art. Van Meegeren's forgery therefore, for all its aesthetic merits, lacks the historical significance that makes Vermeer's work artistically great.

I actually found myself enjoying this passage because I think the author is an idiot. It's fun to disagree. Here, the author goes to great lengths to conclude that *Emmaus*, an original painting by Han van Meegeren in the style of—and with the forged signature of—Dutch master Jan Vermeer, is "inferior as art" even though it is "aesthetically superior." I suppose it depends on your personal definition of art, but to me: What a load of crap.

It won't make you any friends, but on the LSAT you should try to foster this hypercritical attitude in yourself. Above all else, *argue*. You can't argue without taking a position, and taking a position forces you to crystallize concepts in your mind. (Not to mention it's, you know, what you'll be doing every day as an attorney.)

Having taken a position on this passage, you could take my test away from me and I'd still be able to tell you most of what it contains. I wouldn't get every single detail, but I can tell you exactly what the author believes about forgeries as art, and I can tell you specifically why I think he is wrong: He thinks "artistic greatness" requires "vision" whereas I think art, if aesthetically pleasing, can be great even if it's derivative. I'm not bothered if you don't agree with me. In fact, in reality I don't much care about the issue. I don't have to write a rebuttal or anything; the point is to comprehend the passage, and staking out a strong position has helped me do that.

7

QUESTION 7:

Which one of the following most accurately expresses the main point of the passage?

A) *The Disciples at Emmaus*, van Meegeren's forgery of a Vermeer, was a failure in both aesthetic and artistic terms.
B) The aesthetic value of a work of art is less dependent on the work's visible characteristics than on certain intangible characteristics.
C) Forged artworks are artistically inferior to originals because artistic value depends in large part on originality of vision.
D) The most skilled forgers can deceive even highly qualified art experts into accepting their work as original.
E) Art critics tend to be unreliable judges of the aesthetic and artistic quality of works of art.

Main-point questions are extremely common on the LSAT, and you should always be able to come up with *some* kind of an advance answer. You'll rarely be exactly right, but if you can't come up with any advance answer at all then you're definitely doing something wrong. (You probably need to read slower, and experiment with the "take a position" technique discussed above.) Here's my prediction: The author came here to waste our time with the argument that forgeries (like van Meegeren's *Emmaus*) are not great art because they lack vision.

A) The author specifically said *Emmaus* was an aesthetic success, so this isn't the answer.
B) The author's main conclusion wasn't about determining aesthetic value, it was about determining artistic greatness. Next contestant, please.
C) This matches my advance answer nicely, so I'm leaning toward C.
D) The main point wasn't about whether or not forgers can deceive art experts. You might have picked this answer if you'd only read the first paragraph and then let your eyes glaze over, but it's not the main point of the argument as a whole.
E) Again, this would be tempting if you'd only read the first paragraph. But since C matches our advance answer much more closely, we don't have to waste much time to eliminate this answer choice. C is our answer.

QUESTION 8:

The passage provides the strongest support for inferring that Lessing holds which one of the following views?

A) The judgments of critics who pronounced *The Disciples at Emmaus* to be aesthetically superb were not invalidated by the revelation that the painting is a forgery.
B) The financial value of a work of art depends more on its purely aesthetic qualities than on its originality.
C) Museum curators would be better off not taking art critics' opinions into account when attempting to determine whether a work of art is authentic.
D) Because it is such a skilled imitation of Vermeer, *The Disciples at Emmaus* is as artistically successful as are original paintings by artists who are less significant than Vermeer.
E) Works of art that have little or no aesthetic value can still be said to be great achievements in artistic terms.

Don't Stress Over Inferences

Be careful when you see the word "infer." Usually, little to no inference is actually required—you definitely don't have to be Sherlock Holmes. Here, if one of the answer choices is something the author explicitly attributes to Lessing, that's the answer.

There's no way to answer this question in advance. Instead, we have to evaluate the answer choices and figure out which one Lessing would agree with or—preferably—has already said in the passage.

A) Starting in line 29, the author says Lessing acknowledges *Emmaus*'s aesthetic qualities. So A looks good off the bat.
B) The passage says little, if anything, about the financial value of artworks. I don't see how this can be the answer.
C) The author attributes no opinion regarding the authentication of artworks to Lessing.
D) Lessing believes that *Emmaus* is *less* artistically successful than Vermeer's works, and offers no opinion on artists who are less successful than Vermeer.
E) The passage, including all opinions attributed to Lessing, is about works of art that *do* have aesthetic value. We have no way of knowing what Lessing thinks about works *without* aesthetic value. Our answer is A.

QUESTION 9:

In the first paragraph, the author refers to a highly reputed critic's persistence in believing van Meegeren's forgery to be a genuine Vermeer primarily in order to

A) argue that many art critics are inflexible in their judgments
B) indicate that the critics who initially praised The Disciples at Emmaus were not as knowledgeable as they appeared
C) suggest that the painting may yet turn out to be a genuine Vermeer
D) emphasize that the concept of forgery itself is internally incoherent
E) illustrate the difficulties that skillfully executed forgeries can pose for art critics

When a question asks us why an author used a particular part of his argument, it's critical that we try to answer the question before we go to the answer choices. My advance answer here is: "The author used the critic's persistence as an illustration of how difficult it is to tell the difference between a genuine work of art and a forgery."

A) This doesn't match my advance answer. The author's main point (eventually) was not that art critics are inflexible, but that artistic greatness requires something more than aesthetics. This isn't the answer.
B) The author's intention wasn't to slam art critics. The author used the example about the art critic as a foundation for his eventual conclusion that art requires vision. This isn't the answer either.

C) The author certainly does not believe that *Emmaus* could actually be genuine. Quite the opposite.

D) I don't even know what this answer choice is supposed to mean. Why would "the concept of forgery" be "internally incoherent"? I'm really hoping the answer is E.

E) Exactly! This matches my advance answer and has to be correct. E is our answer.

QUESTION 10:

10

The reaction described in which one of the following scenarios is most analogous to the reaction of the art critics mentioned in line 13?

A) lovers of a musical group contemptuously reject a tribute album recorded by various other musicians as a second-rate imitation

B) art historians extol the work of a little-known painter as innovative until it is discovered that the painter lived much more recently than was originally thought

C) diners at a famous restaurant effusively praise the food as delicious until they learn that the master chef is away for the night

D) literary critics enthusiastically applaud a new novel until its author reveals that its central symbols are intended to represent political views that the critics dislike

E) movie fans evaluate a particular movie more favorably than they otherwise might have because their favorite actor plays the lead role

The art critics mentioned in line 13 were embarrassed when it was revealed that *Emmaus* was not really a Vermeer after they had raved about the painting's greatness. So in the correct answer, I'm looking for a group (maybe a group of "experts") whose judgment turns out to be embarrassingly wrong.

A) Nope. Lovers of a musical group don't have to be embarrassed when other musicians pay "tribute" by butchering their songs.

B) I'm very skeptical of this answer since it's about art historians—too close to the subject matter at hand. Beware of such traps for the lazy. The new information revealed here (that the painter had lived more recently than thought) might change the art historians' position on whether the painting was innovative, but they wouldn't necessarily be embarrassed as a result. I don't think this can be our answer.

C) Definitely a potential answer. If diners rave about a meal until they learn that a famous chef actually didn't cook the meal, then they have changed their tune without a substantive reason for doing so. They loved the food five minutes ago; why don't they love it now?

D) Discovering that the author of a book you previously loved has political views opposite to your own could be a decent reason to stop praising the book. Not awful, but C is better, so this is out.

E) Movie fans are perfectly justified in loving movies that feature their favorite actors. Our answer is C.

11

QUESTION 11:

The passage provides the strongest support for inferring that Lessing holds which one of the following views?

A) It is probable that many paintings currently hanging in important museums are actually forgeries.
B) The historical circumstances surrounding the creation of a work are important in assessing the artistic value of that work.
C) The greatness of an innovative artist depends on how much influence he or she has on other artists.
D) The standards according to which a work is judged to be a forgery tend to vary from one historical period to another.
E) An artist who makes use of techniques developed by others cannot be said to be innovative.

There's no way to answer in advance here, so we're back to evaluating all five choices to find the one that Lessing agrees with. Again, we're hopefully going to find something that he said, explicitly, in the passage. Remember Lessing's main idea (which seems to be adopted by the author of the passage): Great art requires more than just aesthetics—it also requires "vision."

A) This isn't related to the main point of the passage, or Lessing's role in the passage, so I doubt it's the correct answer.
B) This seems pretty good. Lessing would care about "historical circumstances" because he cares whether an artist was the first to use a certain style or technique. This is our answer unless something better jumps out at us. (Note that "historical circumstances" is a very broad category. It's easy to make a case that Lessing would care, at least somewhat, about historical circumstances.)
C) Influence on other artists isn't mentioned anywhere in the passage. This is not a good answer.
D) This isn't related to the main point of the passage.
E) This goes a step too far. I'm pretty sure Lessing would be okay with the claim that artists inspired or taught by other artists could still be innovative. On some level, aren't they all? Our answer is B.

12

QUESTION 12:

The passage most strongly supports which one of the following statements?

A) In any historical period, the criteria by which a work is classified as a forgery can be a matter of considerable debate.
B) An artist who uses techniques that others have developed is most likely a forger.
C) A successful forger must originate a new artistic vision.
D) Works of art created early in the career of a great artist are more likely than those created later to embody historic innovations.
E) A painting can be a forgery even if it is not a copy of a particular original work of art.

Again, no advance answer. Let's just keep the main point in mind while running through all five answer choices.

A) This is probably true, but it's not the point of the passage, so I don't think it's our answer.
B) Most artists probably use techniques that were developed by others. This is certainly not the answer.
C) The passage doesn't really say anything about being a "successful forger." In fact, it doesn't seem like the author would even agree that there's any such thing. So this is eliminated for sure.

D) The passage takes no position on whether artists get more or less innovative as they age, so this can't be right.

E) This must be true according to the passage. *Emmaus* wasn't a copy of a painting... it was a copy of a style, with a forged signature. Let's go with E.

QUESTION 13:

Which one of the following, if true, would most strengthen Lessing's contention that a painting can display aesthetic excellence without possessing an equally high degree of artistic value?

A) Many of the most accomplished art forgers have had moderately successful careers as painters of original works.

B) Reproductions painted by talented young artists whose traditional training consisted in the copying of masterpieces were often seen as beautiful, but never regarded as great art.

C) While experts can detect most forgeries, they can be duped by a talented forger who knows exactly what characteristics experts expect to find in the work of a particular painter.

D) Most attempts at art forgery are ultimately unsuccessful because the forger has not mastered the necessary techniques.

E) The criteria by which aesthetic excellence is judged change significantly from one century to another and from one culture to another.

When I read the passage, I disagreed with Lessing's assertion that a painting can display aesthetic excellence without possessing high artistic value. (I think he's being pretentious.) Not to worry. Since I reacted to his argument—disagreeing is better than having no opinion at all—I should be well-equipped to strengthen it. I think a definition of "artistic value" would really help here. Something like "artistic value requires more than just aesthetics" might be a good start. I know that's basically his conclusion, but if it were true, then his conclusion would also be true.

A) It seems like this would hurt Lessing's cause, if anything. It's out.

B) This is an example of how something can be aesthetically pleasing, but not regarded as great art. It's probably going to turn out to be the answer.

C) The fact that forgers can so easily dupe experts can only hurt Lessing's case, since theoretically they're the arbiters of artistic value. This is out.

D) This is irrelevant, so it's out. Nobody has suggested that bad forgeries might be great art. It's *good* forgeries that are problematic.

E) Change is irrelevant too, so this is outta here as well. Our answer is B.

Passage Three (Questions 14-19)

Passage A

One function of language is to influence others'
behavior by changing what they know, believe, or
desire. For humans engaged in conversation, the
perception of another's mental state is perhaps the
(5) most common vocalization stimulus.

While animal vocalizations may have evolved
because they can potentially alter listeners' behavior to
the signaler's benefit, such communication is—in
contrast to human language—inadvertent, because
(10) most animals, with the possible exception of chimpanzees,
cannot attribute mental states to others. The male
Physalaemus frog calls because calling causes females
to approach and other males to retreat, but there is no
evidence that he does so because he attributes knowledge
(15) or desire to other frogs, or because he knows his calls
will affect their knowledge and that this knowledge
will, in turn, affect their behavior. Research also suggests
that, in marked contrast to humans, nonhuman primates
do not produce vocalizations in response to perception
(20) of another's need for information. Macaques, for example,
give alarm calls when predators approach and coo calls
upon finding food, yet experiments reveal no evidence
that individuals were more likely to call about these
events when they were aware of them but their offspring
(25) were clearly ignorant; similarly, chimpanzees do not
appear to adjust their calling to inform ignorant
individuals of their own location or that of food. Many
animal vocalizations whose production initially seems
goal-directed are not as purposeful as they first appear.

Passage B

(30) Many scientists distinguish animal communication
systems from human language on the grounds that the
former are rigid responses to stimuli, whereas human
language is spontaneous and creative.

In this connection, it is commonly stated that no
(35) animal can use its communication system to lie.
Obviously, a lie requires intention to deceive: to judge
whether a particular instance of animal communication
is truly prevarication requires knowledge of the animal's
intentions. Language philosopher H. P. Grice explains
(40) that for an individual to mean something by uttering *x*,
the individual must intend, in expressing *x*, to induce
an audience to believe something and must also intend
the utterance to be recognized as so intended. But
conscious intention is a category of mental experience
(45) widely believed to be uniquely human. Philosopher
Jacques Maritain's discussion of the honeybee's
elaborate "waggle-dance" exemplifies this view.
Although bees returning to the hive communicate to
other bees the distance and direction of food sources,
(50) such communication is, Maritain asserts, merely a
conditioned reflex: animals may use communicative
signs but lack conscious intention regarding their use.

But these arguments are circular: conscious
intention is ruled out a priori and then its absence
(55) taken as evidence that animal communication is
fundamentally different from human language. In fact,
the narrowing of the perceived gap between animal
communication and human language revealed by
recent research with chimpanzees and other animals
(60) calls into question not only the assumption that the
difference between animal and human communication
is qualitative rather than merely quantitative, but also
the accompanying assumption that animals respond
mechanically to stimuli, whereas humans speak with
(65) conscious understanding and intent.

Comparative reading was added to the LSAT in June of 2007. I find it slightly more
interesting than the other reading comprehension passages because you get two
short pieces rather than one longer one. As I read—especially as I read Passage B—
I'm going to consider how Passage B relates to Passage A. Does it agree? Disagree?
Or relate in some other way?

Passage A is about language used as communication. According to this selection,
both humans and other animals use language to communicate information (about
a looming predator, perhaps) to other animals. However, according to the passage,
nonhuman animals can't grasp that other animals don't know the information they
are expressing, because animals "cannot attribute mental states to others." This is
puzzling. If a macaque doesn't know that the other macaques don't see the leopard,
then why does the macaque give an alarm call? Passage A provides no answer to this
question. Maybe Passage B will shed some light?

Passage B starts by providing another example of nonhuman animals apparently
communicating by accident: Honeybees dance to give directions to food sources
even though they lack conscious intention to communicate. But in line 53, Passage B
takes an abrupt turn. The author dismisses as circular the logic behind the honeybee
example: According to the author of Passage B, philosophers have only *assumed*
that honeybees and other animals lack conscious intent to communicate. The au-

thor of Passage B talks about the "narrowing of the perceived gap between animal communication and human language" and leaves open the possibility that animals actually do communicate with conscious intent. So maybe Passage A and Passage B disagree on this point. Passage A says "animals lack the conscious intent to communicate," while Passage B isn't so sure.

QUESTION 14:

14

Both passages are primarily concerned with addressing which one of the following questions?

A) Are animals capable of deliberately prevaricating in order to achieve specific goals?
B) Are the communications of animals characterized by conscious intention?
C) What kinds of stimuli are most likely to elicit animal vocalizations?
D) Are the communication systems of nonhuman primates qualitatively different from those of all other animals?
E) Is there a scientific consensus about the differences between animal communication systems and human language?

We're asked to identify the main topic of both passages. Our advance answer is "both passages are concerned with whether or not nonhuman animals have a conscious intent to communicate." Note that any answer choice will have to be something discussed by *both* passages, not just one.

A) Prevarication isn't mentioned in Passage A, so this is out.
B) This almost exactly matches our advance answer, so it's the frontrunner.
C) This is mentioned in Passage A, but it's not the "primary concern" of either passage.
D) Of course human communication systems are qualitatively different from those of all other animals. Honeybees don't use voices to speak, much less use a human language. This wasn't the concern of either passage, so it's out.
E) Passage B does discuss whether there is a scientific consensus, but Passage A doesn't address this at all. It's out. Our answer has to be B.

QUESTION 15:

15

In discussing the philosopher Maritain, the author of passage B seeks primarily to

A) describe an interpretation of animal communication that the author believes rests on a logical error
B) suggest by illustration that there is conscious intention underlying the communicative signs employed by certain animals
C) present an argument in support of the view that animal communication systems are spontaneous and creative
D) furnish specific evidence against the theory that most animal communication is merely a conditioned reflex
E) point to a noted authority on animal communication whose views the author regards with respect

The author of Passage B introduced Maritain to use him as a counterpoint. So any answer I choose will have to include some sort of disagreement.

A) "Logical error" indicates disagreement. This is probably the answer.
B) The author did eventually suggest that there might be conscious intention, but he didn't use Maritain in order to make this suggestion. Also, no mention of disagreement with Maritain. This is out.
C) This answer doesn't mention any disagreement with Maritain. See ya.
D) No mention of disagreement with Maritain, so it's out.
E) This answer choice doesn't mention disagreement, nor was Maritain a noted authority on animal communication. No way. Our answer is A.

16

QUESTION 16:

The author of passage B would be most likely to agree with which one of the following statements regarding researchers who subscribe to the position articulated in passage A?

A) They fail to recognize that humans often communicate without any clear idea of their listeners' mental states.
B) Most of them lack the credentials needed to assess the relevant experimental evidence correctly.
C) They ignore well-known evidence that animals do in fact practice deception.
D) They make assumptions about matters that should be determined empirically.
E) They falsely believe that all communication systems can be explained in terms of their evolutionary benefits.

The author of Passage B seems to disagree with the researchers in Passage A who believe that animals lack consciousness of their listeners' mental states when they communicate. We'll look for that general sentiment as we head into the answer choices.

A) Nothing in the passages mentions humans communicating without a clear sense of their listeners. I don't see any evidence for this answer, so I don't think it can be the right one.
B) The author of Passage B definitely does not question the researchers' credentials. This is easy to eliminate.
C) Nothing about deception in Passage A, so this is out.
D) In lines 53–56, Passage B says that the researchers who believe animals lack conscious intent to communicate are ruling it out "a priori"—in other words, they are *assuming* it. This seems pretty good.
E) Don't see any evidence for this answer choice. We have to go with D.

Find Your Pace

Experiment with your pacing on the Logical Reasoning sections. Most students don't finish in the allotted 35 minutes. That's okay! Some folks who *do* finish probably shouldn't; they compromise too much accuracy in pursuit of speed. The only way to find your optimal pacing is to experiment. Next time you do a practice test, see what happens if you only try to answer 20 questions in 35 minutes, and guess on the rest. (Remember that you'll guess correctly on one out of five questions.) What if you only attempt 15? Eventually, you'll find the pacing that's right for you.

17

QUESTION 17:

Which one of the following assertions from passage A provides support for the view attributed to Maritain in passage B (lines 50–52)?

A) One function of language is to influence the behavior of others by changing what they think.
B) Animal vocalizations may have evolved because they have the potential to alter listeners' behavior to the signaler's benefit.
C) It is possible that chimpanzees may have the capacity to attribute mental states to others.
D) There is no evidence that the male *Physalaemus* frog calls because he knows that his calls will affect the knowledge of other frogs.
E) Macaques give alarm calls when predators approach and coo calls upon finding food.

Maritain believed animals lack conscious intent to communicate. Passage A mentions a lot of support for this position. The most prominent examples in Passage A were the frogs in line 12 and the macaques in line 20. One of these could be the answer.

A) Not what I'm looking for. I'm looking for frogs or macaques.
B) Not what I'm looking for.
C) This would go *against* Maritain's position, so it's out for sure.
D) This is specifically mentioned in Passage A, and it supports Maritain's view that animals lack conscious intent to communicate, so it's our best guess thus far.
E) This is specifically mentioned in Passage A but it does *not* support Maritain's view so it's out. Our answer is D.

QUESTION 18:

The authors would be most likely to disagree over

A) the extent to which communication among humans involves the ability to perceive the mental states of others
B) the importance of determining to what extent animal communication systems differ from human language
C) whether human language and animal communication differ from one another qualitatively or merely in a matter of degree
D) whether chimpanzees' vocalizations suggest that they may possess the capacity to attribute mental states to others
E) whether animals' vocalizations evolved to alter the behavior of other animals in a way that benefits the signaler

The authors seem to disagree on whether nonhuman animals have a conscious intent to influence the minds of others when they communicate. That's our advance answer.

A) This is about humans, so it's out.
B) They aren't arguing about the *importance* of the issue—they're arguing about the issue itself. This is out.
C) This one sounds good because Passage A posits a qualitative difference (humans have intention; animals don't), while Passage B specifically asks whether the difference is qualitative rather than merely quantitative (starting in line 60).
D) It seems likely that the authors would disagree about whether chimps have the capacity to attribute mental states to others. Passage B only mentions a "narrowing of the perceived gap" between human language and the communication of "chimpanzees and other animals." This is pretty tough to pass up, but it's just too much of a stretch. C is still better supported by the evidence.
E) Both authors would agree that animals influence the behavior of others. This is out. Our best answer is C.

QUESTION 19:

Passage B differs from passage A in that passage B is more

A) optimistic regarding the ability of science to answer certain fundamental questions
B) disapproving of the approach taken by others writing on the same general topic
C) open-minded in its willingness to accept the validity of apparently conflicting positions
D) supportive of ongoing research related to the question at hand
E) circumspect in its refusal to commit itself to any positions with respect to still-unsettled research questions

By now we see that all of the questions in this section are essentially the same. If you got the main point of Passage A (nonhuman animals lack conscious intention to influence the minds of others when they communicate) and the main point of Passage B (science hasn't proven this yet, and it's possible that animals *do* have such conscious intent) then you can answer almost every question.

A) I don't think this is it. If anything, Passage A is "more optimistic regarding the ability of science"—Passage A seems to believe that science has already proven nonhuman animals don't consciously attempt to influence the minds of others. Passage B doesn't think the picture is quite so clear. We want something better.
B) Passage B does disapprove of the approach taken by Maritain and others. I didn't immediately love this one, but it's probably the correct answer.
C) I don't see how Passage B is more "open-minded" than Passage A.
D) Both passages seem equally supportive of research.
E) "Circumspect" indicates that Passage B is shady in some way. It's not shady to refuse to commit to a position until research is complete; quite the opposite, in fact. There's no way this is the answer, so our answer must be B.

Passage Four (Questions 20–27)

In contrast to the mainstream of U.S. historiography during the late nineteenth and early twentieth centuries, African American historians of the period, such as George Washington Williams and

(5) W. E. B. DuBois, adopted a transnational perspective. This was true for several reasons, not the least of which was the necessity of doing so if certain aspects of the history of African Americans in the United States were to be treated honestly.

(10) First, there was the problem of citizenship. Even after the adoption in 1868 of the Fourteenth Amendment to the U.S. Constitution, which defined citizenship, the question of citizenship for African Americans had not been genuinely resolved. Because

(15) of this, emigrationist sentiment was a central issue in black political discourse, and both issues were critical topics for investigation. The implications for historical scholarship and national identity were enormous. While some black leaders insisted on their right to U.S.

(20) citizenship, others called on black people to emigrate and find a homeland of their own. Most African Americans were certainly not willing to relinquish their claims to the benefits of U.S. citizenship, but many had reached a point of profound pessimism and had

(25) begun to question their allegiance to the United States.

Mainstream U.S. historiography was firmly rooted in a nationalist approach during this period; the glorification of the nation and a focus on the nation-state as a historical force were dominant. The

(30) expanding spheres of influence of Europe and the United States prompted the creation of new genealogies of nations, new myths about the inevitability of nations, their "temperaments," their destinies. African American intellectuals who

(35) confronted the nationalist approach to historiography were troubled by its implications. Some argued that imperialism was a natural outgrowth of nationalism and its view that a state's strength is measured by the extension of its political power over colonial territory;

(40) the scramble for colonial empires was a distinct aspect of nationalism in the latter part of the nineteenth century.

Yet, for all their distrust of U.S. nationalism, most early black historians were themselves engaged in a

(45) sort of nation building. Deliberately or not, they contributed to the formation of a collective identity, reconstructing a glorious African past for the purposes of overturning degrading representations of blackness and establishing a firm cultural basis for a

(50) shared identity. Thus, one might argue that black historians' internationalism was a manifestation of a kind of nationalism that posits a diasporic community, which, while lacking a sovereign territory or official language, possesses a single culture, however

(55) mythical, with singular historical roots. Many members of this diaspora saw themselves as an oppressed "nation" without a homeland, or they imagined Africa as home. Hence, these historians understood their task to be the writing of the history

(60) of a people scattered by force and circumstance, a history that began in Africa.

The first paragraph of this passage starts off with a lot of pompous language that is really off-putting to me. "Historiography"? "A transnational perspective"? This really sucks. I'm not going to be actually interested here, so I have to play *Why are you wasting my time with this?* in order to stay awake. So, chip firmly on my shoulder, I query the author at the end of the first paragraph.

It seems as if the author is wasting my time because he wants to tell me that a "transnational perspective" (no clue what that means just yet) was necessary in order to treat the history of African-Americans honestly. For now, I'm assuming that the douchebaggy term "historiography" just means "history." OK, fine, I'm with you so far.

The second paragraph seems to be an example of one of the problems with African-American history. The author says some Black leaders encouraged African-Americans to emigrate to other countries, but many Blacks were reticent to renounce their U.S. citizenship.

The third paragraph is about the nationalism prevalent in the "historiography" (I'm starting to think this means something like "written history") of the late 19th and early 20th centuries. Black historians, says the author, were "troubled" by this nationalism.

The fourth paragraph discusses how early Black historians (surprisingly, the author seems to suggest) engaged in nationalism of their own by creating a glorious history for Blacks that was rooted in Africa. Rather than a country-focused nationalism like U.S. nationalism, this nationalism is the history of a diasporic community without a homeland but possessing a singular culture.

Unfortunately, my grasp of the passage on the whole is shaky at best. I think the main point is "Black historians created a diasporic nationalism for African-Americans as a counter to the U.S. nationalism of the time" but I am 1) not entirely sure what that means and 2) really struggling to stay awake. Because it's so focused on academia, this is an extremely difficult passage for me. I just don't see the real-world significance. I'm in trouble here, and it is devastating that there are *eight* questions for this passage. Not a good passage to misunderstand. But let's take our hypothesis into the questions and see what we can do.

QUESTION 20:

20

Which one of the following most accurately expresses the main idea of the passage?

A) Historians are now recognizing that the major challenge faced by African Americans in the late nineteenth and early twentieth centuries was the struggle for citizenship.

B) Early African American historians who practiced a transnational approach to history were primarily interested in advancing an emigrationist project.

C) U.S. historiography in the late nineteenth and early twentieth centuries was characterized by a conflict between African American historians who viewed history from a transnational perspective and mainstream historians who took a nationalist perspective.

D) The transnational perspective of early African American historians countered mainstream nationalist historiography, but it was arguably nationalist itself to the extent that it posited a culturally unified diasporic community.

E) Mainstream U.S. historians in the late nineteenth and early twentieth centuries could no longer justify their nationalist approach to history once they were confronted with the transnational perspective taken by African American historians.

This is a main-point question. Our advance answer was "Black historians created a diasporic nationalism for African-Americans as a counter to the U.S. nationalism of the time." We may not find that in the answer choices, but hopefully if we can figure out the correct answer by process of elimination, we can then use that answer to learn a bit more about what the passage was supposed to mean.

A) This is definitely not what the passage is about. The passage was an analysis of early Black historians, not the historians of today. This is out.

B) The passage doesn't say that early Black historians advocated for emigration. The passage attributes emigrationist policies only to some Black leaders. So this is also out.

C) No, African American historians actually created their own nationalist perspective according to the last paragraph.

D) This has to be it. It follows along with my paragraph-by-paragraph analysis above, and from now on we can use it when we need to consider the main point of the passage. This is a rare example of a question actually teaching you something.

E) The main point of the passage was about Black historians, not mainstream historians. D is the best answer.

21

QUESTION 21:

Which one of the following phrases most accurately conveys the sense of the word "reconstructing" as it is used in line 47?

A) correcting a misconception about
B) determining the sequence of events in
C) investigating the implications of
D) rewarding the promoters of
E) shaping a conception of

Let's go back to the beginning of the third paragraph to get some context. It seems like the word "reconstructing" was meant to be a lot like "inventing." So that's our advance answer.

A) I don't think there were any misconceptions mentioned in the passage.
B) There was nothing in there about putting events in order either.
C) "Investigating" is not invention so this doesn't look right. I'm still looking for something more like my advance answer, something that involves invention or creation.
D) Nope, still looking for invention or creation.
E) This is the only answer close to our advance answer. If you're "shaping a conception," you're inventing or creating a story. I'm still feeling uncomfortable about my grip on the passage, but we have to put our money on E.

22

QUESTION 22:

Which one of the following is most strongly supported by the passage?

A) Emigrationist sentiment would not have been as strong among African Americans in the late nineteenth century had the promise of U.S. citizenship been fully realized for African Americans at that time.
B) Scholars writing the history of diasporic communities generally do not discuss the forces that initially caused the scattering of the members of those communities.
C) Most historians of the late nineteenth and early twentieth centuries endeavored to make the histories of the nations about which they wrote seem more glorious than they actually were.
D) To be properly considered nationalist, a historical work must ignore the ways in which one nation's foreign policy decisions affected other nations.
E) A considerable number of early African American historians embraced nationalism and the inevitability of the dominance of the nation-state.

We can't answer in advance here. We just have to look for an answer choice that (ideally) has been specifically stated in the passage.

A) This seems pretty good. Lines 18–21 say that some Black leaders were calling for full citizenship, while others were calling for emigration. So if full citizenship were given to African-Americans, maybe the call for emigration would have been diminished. This is our answer unless we see something better.
B) There's nothing in the passage that supports this idea.
C) This is hard to prove because it says "most" historians. The passage doesn't provide evidence of what "most" historians were doing. I'm taking a bit of a risk here, but I have to take some calculated risks on the answer choices in order to save time. (Note that this is NOT the same thing as rushing through the passage.) Because I liked A, and because C is a bit iffy, C is out.
D) I don't think the passage gives a definition of what is and what is not "properly called nationalist." So this answer is out.
E) If this answer stopped after "nationalism" we might give it a chance, but when it goes on with "and the inevitability of the nation-state," it goes too far. Our answer is A.

QUESTION 23:

As it is described in the passage, the transnational approach employed by African American historians working in the late nineteenth and early twentieth centuries would be best exemplified by a historical study that

A) investigated the extent to which European and U.S. nationalist mythologies contradicted one another
B) defined the national characters of the United States and several European nations by focusing on their treatment of minority populations rather than on their territorial ambitions
C) recounted the attempts by the United States to gain control over new territories during the late nineteenth and early twentieth centuries
D) considered the impact of emigrationist sentiment among African Americans on U.S. foreign policy in Africa during the late nineteenth century
E) examined the extent to which African American culture at the turn of the century incorporated traditions that were common to a number of African cultures

I think the "transnationalist approach" discussed in the passage is the practice of early Black historians to create a Black nationalism with roots not tied to any specific country, but coming from many different places and originally rooted in Africa. (It's still a bit hazy, but I'm doing my best here.) So let's look for a study that exemplifies that approach.

A) This isn't what we're looking for, and doesn't seem to be what the passage is about.
B) Again, not what we're looking for, and also not what the passage seems to be about.
C) Same explanation as A and B.
D) The passage touched on emigrationist sentiment, but this isn't what the "transnationalist approach" is about.
E) This is the best answer because it's about incorporating traditions of African cultures. It's closest to our advance answer, so let's pick it and move on.

24

QUESTION 24:

The passage provides information sufficient to answer which one of the following questions?

A) Which African nations did early African American historians research in writing their histories of the African diaspora?

B) What were some of the African languages spoken by the ancestors of the members of the African diasporic community who were living in the United States in the late nineteenth century?

C) Over which territories abroad did the United States attempt to extend its political power in the latter part of the nineteenth century?

D) Are there textual ambiguities in the Fourteenth Amendment that spurred the conflict over U.S. citizenship for African Americans?

E) In what ways did African American leaders respond to the question of citizenship for African Americans in the latter part of the nineteenth century?

Here, we're looking for a question that the passage has explicitly answered. (That's what it means for the passage to have provided "sufficient" information to answer a question.)

A) There is no mention of specific African nations, so this is out.

B) There is no mention of specific African languages, so this is gone.

C) There is no mention of specific colonial territory, so this won't work.

D) There is no mention of specific 14th Amendment text, so this is out. I really hope the answer is E.

E) Phew. The passage says that African-American leaders responded to the question of citizenship with demands for citizenship and with outcries for emigration. This is our answer.

25

QUESTION 25:

The author of the passage would be most likely to agree with which one of the following statements?

A) Members of a particular diasporic community have a common country of origin.

B) Territorial sovereignty is not a prerequisite for the project of nation building.

C) Early African American historians who rejected nationalist historiography declined to engage in historical myth-making of any kind.

D) The most prominent African American historians in the late nineteenth and early twentieth centuries advocated emigration for African Americans.

E) Historians who employed a nationalist approach focused on entirely different events from those studied and written about by early African American historians.

We can't answer in advance here, but let's remember the main point as taught to us by Question 20: "The transnational perspective of early African-American historians countered mainstream nationalist historiography, but it was arguably nationalist itself to the extent that it posited a culturally unified diasporic community."

A) The author might disagree with this. There was no specific country of origin mentioned, rather, an entire continent.

B) I think the author would agree with this. Early Black historians built a diasporic cultural nation of African-Americans, even though African-Americans had no territory of their own. This is our answer until something better comes along.

C) We don't know anything at all about historians who "rejected nationalist historiography." This is out.

D) The passage makes no mention of the specific actions of the "most prominent" historians. No way.

E) There's nothing in the passage about some historians focusing on certain events and some focusing on others. We have to stick with B.

QUESTION 26:

The main purpose of the second paragraph of the passage is to

A) explain why early African American historians felt compelled to approach historiography in the way that they did
B) show that governmental actions such as constitutional amendments do not always have the desired effect
C) support the contention that African American intellectuals in the late nineteenth century were critical of U.S. imperialism
D) establish that some African American political leaders in the late nineteenth century advocated emigration as an alternative to fighting for the benefits of U.S. citizenship
E) argue that the definition of citizenship contained in the Fourteenth Amendment to the U.S. Constitution is too limited

The second paragraph was about how some Black leaders called for full citizenship, and some Black leaders encouraged African-Americans to emigrate to other countries, though many Blacks were reluctant to renounce their U.S. citizenship. This was all presented in a passage that, as a whole, discussed the actions of Black historians.

A) This answer works because it seems as if the purpose of including the citizenship controversy was to explain why historians did what they did. I'm hoping all the other answers are terrible so we can pick A.
B) The passage wasn't about governmental actions, so this is out.
C) The second paragraph was not about intellectuals challenging imperialism, so my wishes are coming true.
D) OK, this did happen in the second paragraph, so it's not a terrible choice. But I like answer A more because it's closer to the purpose of the passage as a whole, rather than just a part of it.
E) There was no such argument in the second paragraph, so this is out. Our answer is A.

QUESTION 27:

As it is presented in the passage, the approach to history taken by mainstream U.S. historians of the late nineteenth and early twentieth centuries is most similar to the approach exemplified in which one of the following?

A) An elected official writes a memo suggesting that because a particular course of action has been successful in the past, the government should continue to pursue that course of action.
B) A biographer of a famous novelist argues that the precocity apparent in certain of the novelist's early achievements confirms that her success was attributable to innate talent.
C) A doctor maintains that because a certain medication was developed expressly for the treatment of an illness, it is the best treatment for that illness.
D) A newspaper runs a series of articles in order to inform the public about the environmentally hazardous practices of a large corporation.
E) A scientist gets the same result from an experiment several times and therefore concludes that its chemical reactions always proceed in the observed fashion.

The passage mentioned the glorifying nationalist approach taken by mainstream historians of the period. So we're looking for something similar to that: ideally, people portraying themselves, or their group, or their home football team, or whatever, as glorious and incapable of doing wrong.

A) This isn't self-glorifying, so it's out.
B) This is close. My only concern is that the biographer is glorifying someone else. I'd prefer if the biographer were glorifying herself, or her grandfather or something. Not a bad answer, but not perfect. Let's see what else we've got.
C) This isn't self-glorifying, so no go.
D) Not self-glorifying enough.
E) This isn't self-glorifying, so it's out. Even though B isn't perfect, it's the best answer by far, so we can confidently choose B.

SECTION TWO

Logical Reasoning

(Or: If You're Not Outraged, You're Not Paying Attention)

Before we begin, two quick lessons on logical reasoning.

First, the questions get harder as each section progresses. Most people can't finish the sections without compromising accuracy. If this is you, then guessing on a few questions at the end is a perfectly sound strategy. Take your time and get the early—and more answerable—questions right, because the later ones are going to be very difficult no matter how much time you devote to them.

Second, take a supercritical mindset as you read these arguments, because most of them are (intentionally) horribly flawed. You're essentially being tested on your ability to notice when someone is making a foolish or deceitful argument. The stronger the argument is stated, the more likely it is to be total crap.

Once when I was young, I heard a preacher shout, "*Obviously* a fish didn't just suddenly have legs pop out its sides and start walking up the beach, so clearly, *logically*, the theory of evolution is wrong!" The problem is that no scientist believes in legs popping out the sides of fish, yet virtually all scientists believe in evolution. Yelling, for the preacher, was easier than reading. From that day on, I have been wary of "logical" arguments, especially those that use words like "clearly" or "obviously." On the LSAT, as in real life, as soon as someone presents an argument as "indisputable," you would be wise to dispute it.

Let's dig in, but don't forget to read the Logical Reasoning Question Types for more info on how to spot the patterns and improve your score on these questions.

QUESTION 1:

Mary to Jamal: You acknowledge that as the legitimate owner of this business I have the legal right to sell it whenever I wish. But also you claim that because loyal employees will suffer if I sell it, I therefore have no right to do so. Obviously, your statements taken together are absurd.

Mary's reasoning is most vulnerable to the criticism that she
A) overlooks the possibility that when Jamal claims that she has no right to sell the business, he simply means she has no right to do so at this time
B) overlooks the possibility that her employees also have rights related to the sale of the business
C) provides no evidence for the claim that she does have a right to sell the business
D) overlooks the possibility that Jamal is referring to two different kinds of right
E) attacks Jamal's character rather than his argument

This question, like most questions that ask us to identify a flaw, is very vulnerable to the attacking style that I teach in my classes. Always argue with the speaker! Jamal says Mary has a "legal right" to sell her business, but "no right" to sell her business because her employees will suffer. Life, in other words, is complicated. There's nothing wrong with this.

But Mary is apparently a simpleton. She concludes that Jamal's argument is "absurd" because he acknowledges there are two different kinds of "rights." We need to call bullshit on Mary. My immediate reaction (which, importantly, I arrived at *before* I read the answer choices) was "Mary, there might be a difference between a legal 'right' and a moral 'right.'" Because this advance answer is so strong, we're able to be even more critical than usual when skimming through the answer choices. (Remember: Every answer has only a 20% chance of being correct and an 80% chance of being a professionally written trap.)

A) We can dismiss this answer because of the phrase "at this time." Mary's argument says nothing about selling now vs. later, so this can't be the answer.
B) Mary never goes so far as to conclude that she *does* have a right to sell her business whenever she wishes, so it's not fair to say she has ignored her employees' rights. Just as importantly, this answer simply isn't what we were looking for. Mary's worst flaw was her pathetic attack on Jamal's logic. There's no need to spend more than five seconds on this answer because it doesn't point out Mary's failure.
C) Answers that say "provides no evidence" are almost never correct. Here, Mary points out that Jamal has "already acknowledged" that she has a right. This is evidence, however weak it may be. When an answer says "provides no evidence," make sure that the speaker really has provided *zero* relevant evidence.
D) This answer jumped out at me because it almost exactly matched our advance answer. You won't always able to predict answers so perfectly, but it sure makes life easy when you do. This is our answer unless E really knocks our socks off.
E) Attacking a speaker's character rather than a speaker's argument is a commonly tested flaw on the LSAT, but that's not what Mary does here. This answer would be correct if Mary had said "Jamal, your argument is absurd because you cheat on your girlfriend." Mary does nothing of the sort, so this isn't the answer.

QUESTION 2:

Since there is no survival value in an animal's having an organ that is able to function when all its other organs have broken down to such a degree that the animal dies, it is a result of the efficiency of natural selection that no organ is likely to evolve in such a way that it greatly outlasts the body's other organs.

Of the following, which one illustrates a principle that is most similar to the principle illustrated by the passage?

A) A store in a lower-income neighborhood finds that it is unable to sell its higher-priced goods and so stocks them only when ordered by a customer.
B) The body of an animal with a deficient organ is often able to compensate for that deficiency when other organs perform the task the deficient one normally performs.
C) One car model produced by an automobile manufacturer has a life expectancy that is so much longer than its other models that its great popularity requires the manufacturer to stop producing some of the other models.
D) Athletes occasionally overdevelop some parts of their bodies to such a great extent that other parts of their bodies are more prone to injury as a result.
E) Automotive engineers find that it is not cost-effective to manufacture a given automobile part of such high quality that it outlasts all other parts of the automobile, as doing so would not raise the overall quality of the automobile.

On the LSAT, as in real life, arguments against evolution tend to be based on faith, rather than reason, and arguments in favor of evolution tend to be based on scientific evidence. Here, there isn't really an argument. Instead, it's just one long premise—an interesting fact about natural selection. The passage points out one of the "efficiencies" of natural selection: the fact that most organs tend to break down at approximately the same time, since there would be no point in having working lungs, for example, long after one's heart had stopped beating.

Since there's no argument here, there's no logic to attack. Instead, the question asks us to match this phenomenon with another similar phenomenon. We're looking for "parts wear out simultaneously," since that's what the selection was about.

A) This has nothing to do with parts wearing out so I can't see how it could be the correct answer.
B) What about organs taking over for a failing organ? It's about parts, but it's not about parts wearing out at the same time.
C) This is more like one animal dying before another, rather than parts wearing out before other parts, so it's not this one.
D) This discusses parts being overdeveloped and causing other parts to fail. Again, it's about parts, but it's not about parts wearing out at the same time.
E) This *is* about parts wearing out over time. This is about automotive engineers deciding that it is not cost-effective to create some parts that far outlast the other parts on a car. It's very close to my advance answer, so it's got to be our pick.

QUESTION 3:

Commentator: If a political administration is both economically successful and successful at protecting individual liberties, then it is an overall success. Even an administration that fails to care for the environment may succeed overall if it protects individual liberties. So far, the present administration has not cared for the environment but has successfully protected individual liberties.

If all of the statements above are true, then which one of the following must be true?

A) The present administration is economically successful.
B) The present administration is not an overall success.
C) If the present administration is economically successful, then it is an overall success.
D) If the present administration had been economically successful, it would have cared for the environment.
E) If the present administration succeeds at environmental protection, then it will be an overall success.

The first sentence of the commentator's argument is a premise that states that if a political administration is successful in *both* of two areas (economics and protecting individual liberties) then it is successful overall. The second sentence, about the environment, is completely irrelevant here. If it is economically successful and it protects individual liberties, then according to the commentator it is successful overall regardless of whether it protects the environment. The last sentence tells us that the present administration has not cared for the environment (which is irrelevant) and has successfully protected individual liberties. On the basis of this information, we are asked to identify something else that must be true. The correct answer here must be directly supported by the facts as presented. Outside information and opinions are not allowed.

A) This hasn't been proven. The administration may or may not be economically successful, but we don't know one way or the other.
B) This hasn't been proven either. The administration may or may not be an overall success.
C) This is likely the correct answer. The administration has already satisfied one criterion (protecting individual liberties), so if the administration were also economically successful, the commentator would have to conclude, based on the criteria given, that the administration is successful overall.
D) This answer makes no sense. Like many incorrect answers, this one basically takes terms from the argument, puts them in a blender, and pours you a milkshake of nonsense.
E) This answer is incorrect because, according to the commentator, the environment is irrelevant to an administration's overall success. Let's go with C.

QUESTION 4:

The legislature is considering a proposed bill that would prohibit fishing in Eagle Bay. Despite widespread concern over the economic effect this ban would have on the local fishing industry, the bill should be enacted. The bay has one of the highest water pollution levels in the nation, and a recent study of the bay's fish found that 80 percent of them contained toxin levels that exceed governmental safety standards. Continuing to permit fishing in Eagle Bay could thus have grave effects on public health.

The argument proceeds by presenting evidence that

A) the toxic contamination of fish in Eagle Bay has had grave economic effects on the local fishing industry
B) the moral principle that an action must be judged on the basis of its foreseeable effects is usually correct
C) the opponents of the ban have failed to weigh properly its foreseeable negative effects against its positive ones
D) failure to enact the ban would carry with it unacceptable risks for the public welfare
E) the ban would reduce the level of toxins in the fish in Eagle Bay

This question makes the normative conclusion ("normative" basically means anything that uses the word "should") that a specific bill banning fishing should be enacted. As soon as the argument said "should" my internal critic said "Oh yeah? Why? Prove it to me." The argument then attempted to do so, by talking about water pollution and food safety. This seemed logically sound. We're not asked to change the argument here, or identify any weaknesses. Rather, we're asked to identify a method of reasoning actually used by the argument. On questions like this, we have to be able to find direct support in the passage for any answer choice, otherwise it is incorrect. Ask yourself "Did the argument actually do this?" If not, then the answer is wrong.

A) The argument said the fish are toxic, and it also said the ban on fishing might have adverse economic effects. But it doesn't say the fish toxicity is *causing* any economic effects. So this isn't it.
B) The argument makes no claim about what is "usually" correct. On the basis of this one word, the answer choice is incorrect.
C) The argument presents no evidence about whether the opponents of the ban have weighed pros vs. cons. This is out.
D) The argument presents environmental risks to the public welfare, so this must be the correct answer.
E) The argument doesn't say that a ban on fishing would reduce the toxicity of fish. Our answer is D.

5

QUESTION 5:

Vandenburg: This art museum is not adhering to its purpose. Its founders intended it to devote as much attention to contemporary art as to the art of earlier periods, but its collection of contemporary art is far smaller than its other collections.

Simpson: The relatively small size of the museum's contemporary art collection is appropriate. It's an art museum, not an ethnographic museum designed to collect every style of every period. Its contemporary art collection is small because its curators believe that there is little high-quality contemporary art.

Which one of the following principles, if valid, most helps to justify the reasoning in Simpson's response to Vandenburg?

A) An art museum should collect only works that its curators consider to be of high artistic quality.
B) An art museum should not collect any works that violate the purpose defined by the museum's founders.
C) An art museum's purpose need not be to collect every style of every period.
D) An ethnographic museum's purpose should be defined according to its curators' beliefs.
E) The intentions of an art museum's curators should not determine what is collected by that museum.

Here, we're asked to support Simpson's argument that the relatively small size of the museum's contemporary art collection is appropriate, against Vandenburg's assertion that the museum's founders intended it to devote as much attention to contemporary art as to the art of earlier periods. Anything that helps Simpson, whether a lot or a little, could be the correct answer here. Incorrect answers will either weaken Simpson's argument, be irrelevant, or perhaps strengthen Simpson's argument less than a better answer does. (We'll keep an eye out for those shades of gray.)

A) At first this didn't seem like a great strengthener. But Simpson says the contemporary collection is small because the curators don't believe there's much high-quality contemporary art available. If that's true, and if it's also true that the museum should only collect high-quality work, then they'll likely have less contemporary art.
B) This neither strengthens nor weakens.
C) This is an interesting answer because it does support Simpson's argument. However, it also seems to simply restate one of Simpson's premises, which doesn't really add that much. Right now, A is better, so C is out.
D) This is irrelevant, because Simpson doesn't dispute the museum's purpose, and Simpson specifically says it is *not* an ethnographic museum.
E) This would weaken Simpson's argument and is therefore conclusively wrong. Our answer is A.

QUESTION 6:

Over the last five years, every new major alternative-energy initiative that initially was promised government funding has since seen that funding severely curtailed. In no such case has the government come even close to providing the level of funds initially earmarked for these projects. Since large corporations have made it a point to discourage alternative-energy projects, it is likely that the corporations' actions influenced the government's funding decisions.

Which one of the following, if true, most strengthens the reasoning above?

A) For the past two decades, most alternative-energy initiatives have received little or no government funding.

B) The funding initially earmarked for a government project is always subject to change, given the mechanisms by which the political process operates.

C) The only research projects whose government funding has been severely curtailed are those that large corporations have made it a point to discourage.

D) Some projects encouraged by large corporations have seen their funding severely curtailed over the last five years.

E) All large corporations have made it a point to discourage some forms of research.

This is a cause-and-effect argument. The author concludes that corporations' actions are influencing the government's funding decisions, *i.e.*, causing the government not to fund certain projects. The evidence supporting this assertion is minimal: Corporations have made it a point to discourage alternative-energy projects. The correct answer will probably strengthen the connection between the evidence and the conclusion. The incorrect answers will weaken the argument, be irrelevant, or strengthen the argument less than a better answer.

A) This is irrelevant. It could be a weakener just as easily as it could be a strengthener.

B) This is probably true, but irrelevant.

C) I was skeptical about this answer choice because of the word "research," which isn't used anywhere in the argument. However, if it's true it strengthens the connection between corporations' actions and government decisions. Sometimes you have to pick the best of a bad lot, and this could definitely be one of those instances. Process of elimination is a perfectly acceptable technique on the LSAT. Let's see what D and E have to say, but C looks decent right now.

D) This could only weaken.

E) This is irrelevant. I don't love it, but our answer is C.

QUESTION 7:

Talbert: Chess is beneficial for school-age children. It is enjoyable, encourages foresight and logical thinking, and discourages carelessness, inattention, and impulsiveness. In short, it promotes mental maturity.

Sklar: My objection to teaching chess to children is that it diverts mental activity from something with societal value, such as science, into something that has no societal value.

Talbert's and Sklar's statements provide the strongest support for holding that they disagree with each other over whether

A) chess promotes mental maturity

B) many activities promote mental maturity just as well as chess does

C) chess is socially valuable and science is not

D) children should be taught to play chess

E) children who neither play chess nor study science are mentally immature

Questions 7 and 8 are a nice pair because superficially they look like the same type of question, but they actually create two distinctly different question types. Number 7 tests our ability to figure out exactly what is being disputed, a critical skill in law school and for practicing lawyers. For the correct answer, one person will clearly say "yes" and the other person will clearly say "no." If either speaker fails to take a position on an answer choice, then that answer choice must be incorrect.

A) Talbert says yes but Sklar doesn't take a position on this point. This can't be the answer.

B) Neither speaker takes a position on this point. Can't be this one either.

C) Sklar says no but Talbert doesn't take a position on this point. Nope.

D) Talbert says yes, Sklar says no. This should be the correct answer.

E) Neither speaker takes a position on this point, so it can't be the correct answer. Our answer is D.

8

QUESTION 8:

Marcia: Not all vegetarian diets lead to nutritional deficiencies. Research shows that vegetarians can obtain a full complement of proteins and minerals from nonanimal foods.

Theodora: You are wrong in claiming that vegetarianism cannot lead to nutritional deficiencies. If most people became vegetarians, some of those losing jobs due to the collapse of many meat-based industries would fall into poverty and hence be unable to afford a nutritionally adequate diet.

Theodora's reply to Marcia's argument is most vulnerable to criticism on the grounds that her reply

A) is directed toward disproving a claim that Marcia did not make
B) ignores the results of the research cited by Marcia
C) takes for granted that no meat-based industries will collapse unless most people become vegetarians
D) uses the word "diet" in a nontechnical sense whereas Marcia's argument uses this term in a medical sense
E) takes for granted that people losing jobs in meat-based industries would become vegetarians

Again, please note the differences between Question 7 and Question 8. The questions look the same superficially, but they're dramatically different. This question asks us to find a flaw in Theodora's argument. If you are reading critically, this question can be quite easy. (If you don't read the arguments critically, you can get confused and spend forever in the answer choices.) Marcia starts by saying "not all" vegetarian diets lead to nutritional deficiencies. Theodora's response starts by saying Marcia is wrong in claiming that vegetarianism "cannot" lead to nutritional deficiencies. Ideally, you should be yelling at Theodora at this point: "Theodora, you're not listening! Marcia never claimed that vegetarianism "cannot" cause nutritional deficiencies." If this is your response, you've already answered the question.

A) Boom, right off the bat. Theodora has responded to a claim that Marcia didn't make. We'll still read the rest of the answer choices, but because A is such a great answer, we get to be even more critical than usual of the remaining answers. This should be easy.
B) Theodora didn't address Marcia's evidence, but her primary flaw was in misunderstanding Marcia's conclusion rather than ignoring her evidence. Because A is a more perfect answer, B is out.
C) This answer uses words from the argument in a double-negatived and nonsensical way—it's professionally written to waste your time and confuse you. This answer choice is a stark illustration of why it is so important to attempt to answer the questions *before* looking at the answer choices. The answer choices are not your friends. The correct answer is to be found in the argument.
D) We aren't told what constitutes a "nontechnical" use of a word, or what might be a "medical" use of a word. There's no way to know whether these folks are speaking in different contexts, and if anything it looks like they're in the same context. In short, we'd have to work too hard to explain why this is the correct answer. And we've already seen a good answer in A, so this is out.
E) Again, this answer takes words from the argument, blends them up, and pours them out into an answer choice that might look reasonable, but it doesn't address Theodora's primary flaw (and doesn't even describe something that she did in her argument). Thanks for playing, answer E. Our answer is A.

QUESTION 9:

Musicologist: Classification of a musical instrument depends on the mechanical action through which it produces music. So the piano is properly called a percussion instrument, not a stringed instrument. Even though the vibration of the piano's strings is what makes its sound, the strings are caused to vibrate by the impact of hammers.

Which one of the following most accurately expresses the main conclusion of the musicologist's argument?

A) Musical instruments should be classified according to the mechanical actions through which they produce sound.
B) Musical instruments should not be classified based on the way musicians interact with them.
C) Some people classify the piano as a stringed instrument because of the way the piano produces sound.
D) The piano should be classified as a stringed instrument rather than as a percussion instrument.
E) It is correct to classify the piano as a percussion instrument rather than as a stringed instrument.

To answer conclusion questions, let's go back to our old standby "Why are you wasting my time with this?" Here, the musicologist gives us a strong hint by using the word "so." Frequently, the words "so," "therefore," "consequently," and the like are used to introduce the main conclusion of an argument. Did the musicologist come here to tell us that the piano is properly called a percussion instrument? I believe she did. The rest of the argument seems to support that point (classification depends on the mechanical action used to create music, and the piano uses hammers to make its sound, therefore the piano is properly called a percussion instrument). My advance answer, therefore, is "The piano is properly called a percussion instrument." All we have to do now is skim the answer choices and hopefully the correct answer will jump out at us.

A) Nothing about the piano. The main point wasn't simply about musical instruments—it was about pianos specifically. This isn't what we're looking for.
B) Again, where is the piano?
C) Here's the piano, but the main point wasn't that "some people" classify the piano as a stringed instrument. It was that the piano is "properly" called a *percussion* instrument. This can't be it.
D) Again, the piano is supposedly a percussion instrument so this can't be the answer either.
E) This almost exactly matches my advance answer and is a correct restatement of the main point of the argument. It's our correct answer.

10

QUESTION 10:

In a vast ocean region, phosphorus levels have doubled in the past few decades due to agricultural runoff pouring out of a large river nearby. The phosphorus stimulates the growth of plankton near the ocean surface. Decaying plankton fall to the ocean floor, where bacteria devour them, consuming oxygen in the process. Due to the resulting oxygen depletion, few fish can survive in this region.

Which one of the following can be properly inferred from the information above?

A) The agricultural runoff pouring out of the river contributes to the growth of plankton near the ocean surface.
B) Before phosphorus levels doubled in the ocean region, most fish were able to survive in that region.
C) If agricultural runoff ceased pouring out of the river, there would be no bacteria on the ocean floor devouring decaying plankton.
D) The quantity of agricultural runoff pouring out of the river has doubled in the past few decades.
E) The amount of oxygen in a body of water is in general inversely proportional to the level of phosphorus in that body of water.

The big mistake that most students make when they see a question like this is that they think they have to dig deep and pick up on some tiny clue to find the correct answer. They think that "inferring" something requires a big leap of deductive reasoning. Time and time again, I've watched my students brand the correct answer as "too obvious" and pick something that hasn't been conclusively established—an incorrect answer. The proper approach on a question like this is to look for something, no matter how simple or obvious, that has been conclusively proven *by the facts as they have been presented*. Generally speaking, this type of question is going to prefer a weakly stated answer choice, because it is easier to conclusively prove something weak than to conclusively prove something strong or absolute. Outside information is irrelevant here: Pick the answer choice that has *direct support* from the passage.

A) The passage gives an example of agricultural runoff increasing phosphorus concentrations in the ocean, which stimulate the growth of plankton near the ocean surface. If all this is true, then answer choice A has been conclusively proven by the passage. I bet this is our pick.
B) The argument doesn't prove that fish ever lived in the region in question, so this can't be the correct answer.
C) The argument doesn't prove that the bacteria wouldn't be there without the plankton, so this can't be it.
D) The argument says phosphorus levels have doubled, but doesn't say that agricultural runoff has doubled. Can't be this one.
E) The words "in general" make it almost impossible to pick this answer. The passage has not proven anything "in general"—rather, it has given some very specific information about a narrow set of circumstances. Our answer is A.

11

QUESTION 11:

Psychologists observing a shopping mall parking lot found that, on average, drivers spent 39 seconds leaving a parking space when another car was quietly waiting to enter it, 51 seconds if the driver of the waiting car honked impatiently, but only 32 seconds leaving a space when no one was waiting. This suggests that drivers feel possessive of their parking spaces even when leaving them, and that this possessiveness increases in reaction to indications that another driver wants the space.

Which one of the following, if true, most weakens the reasoning?

A) The more pressure most drivers feel because others are waiting for them to perform maneuvers with their cars, the less quickly they are able to perform them.

B) The amount of time drivers spend entering a parking space is not noticeably affected by whether other drivers are waiting for them to do so, nor by whether those other drivers are honking impatiently.

C) It is considerably more difficult and time-consuming for a driver to maneuver a car out of a parking space if another car waiting to enter that space is nearby.

D) Parking spaces in shopping mall parking lots are unrepresentative of parking spaces in general with respect to the likelihood that other cars will be waiting to enter them.

E) Almost any driver leaving a parking space will feel angry at another driver who honks impatiently, and this anger will influence the amount of time spent leaving the space.

According to the data provided, drivers spend 32 seconds leaving a space when no one is waiting for the space, 39 seconds (slightly longer) if a car is waiting patiently for the space, and 51 seconds (quite a bit longer) if another driver is honking impatiently while waiting for the space. From this data, the author concludes that drivers "feel possessive" of their parking spaces. This is certainly a reasonable explanation of the data, but it's only one potential explanation out of many.

To weaken a cause-and-effect relationship, we can try to do one of three things:

1) **Provide an alternative cause.** If we can prove that a heightened sense of safety among other drivers caused them to back out more slowly, it seriously weakens the author's case for "possessiveness" causing the delay.

2) **Prove the reversal of cause and effect.** This would be something like "possessive drivers drive more slowly," which doesn't make any sense here. But we are very likely to see the reversal of cause and effect on other cause-and-effect questions.

3) **Show that the purported cause is impossible or unlikely.** This would be something like "possessive drivers have never driven (or, even better, *could* never have driven) as slowly as the drivers in the study."

So here, ask yourself: What other potential reasons could there be? What else would cause drivers to back out more slowly when people are waiting? Safety sprung to my mind when I tackled this question. Wouldn't you back out more slowly if someone were waiting behind you? And might you back out even *more* slowly if someone honked while you were backing out? This may not be the exact correct answer, but the correct answer will probably be this or something very similar to it. The argument gave one explanation—the correct answer should give another one.

A) Okay, maybe drivers feel pressure maneuvering their cars when people are watching and waiting for them to back out. This isn't the safety-related explanation I initially came up with, but it's definitely a reasonable one. It fits perfectly with the data, too: if another driver waits patiently you get a little nervous, but if another driver honks at you, impatiently, you get *even more* nervous. If it were true, then it would provide a different (and better) explanation than the author's unsupported "possessiveness" rationale. Sounds like a winner.

B) Since this answer is about how drivers perform while entering (not exiting) a space, it's a stretch to make it the correct answer. Because we've already read A, which is a good, straightforward weakener, we can eliminate B from consideration.

C) This would be a good answer if A were not present. The reason it's not as good as A, in my mind, is that it doesn't explain why people take even longer to back out when another driver honks as they do if the other driver just sits there patiently. (The honking should be irrelevant to the actual maneuvering, absent the pressure factor described in A.) A is still better.

D) This answer, if it were true, wouldn't strengthen or weaken the argument. Move along.

E) This answer explains why people take longer when honked at, but doesn't explain why people take longer when another driver waits patiently for their space. It's not as good as our answer, A.

QUESTION 12:

Shark teeth are among the most common vertebrate fossils; yet fossilized shark skeletons are much less common—indeed, comparatively rare among fossilized vertebrate skeletons.

Which one of the following, if true, most helps to resolve the apparent paradox described above?

A) Unlike the bony skeletons of other vertebrates, shark skeletons are composed of cartilage, and teeth and bone are much more likely to fossilize than cartilage is.
B) The rare fossilized skeletons of sharks that are found are often found in areas other than those in which fossils of shark teeth are plentiful.
C) Fossils of sharks' teeth are quite difficult to distinguish from fossils of other kinds of teeth.
D) Some species of sharks alive today grow and lose many sets of teeth during their lifetimes.
E) The physical and chemical processes involved in the fossilization of sharks' teeth are as common as those involved in the fossilization of shark skeletons.

A "paradox" is a set of circumstances that can't simultaneously be true. In *Back to the Future*, Marty McFly can't be the son of George McFly and Lorraine Baines if he goes back in time and accidentally prevents the two from falling in love. This would be a real paradox, so he does everything he can to prevent it. On the LSAT, we are never presented with real paradoxes, only apparent paradoxes that have reasonable explanations. Our job is to figure out an explanation that allows both sides of the so-called paradox to be true simultaneously.

Here, we're presented with a puzzling situation: How can it be that shark teeth are among the most common vertebrate fossils, but shark skeletons are comparatively rare among fossilized vertebrate skeletons? The correct answer here will explain how this is possible, and leave us with an understanding that there really isn't a paradox at all. (Incorrect answers will either not explain the paradox, *i.e.*, be irrelevant, or they will actually make the paradox even harder to understand.)

Before looking at the answer choices, I'm thinking there must be some difference between shark teeth and shark skeletons. If shark teeth are unusually unlikely to decompose but the skeletons are not, that would be a good explanation. Alternatively, shark skeletons could be unusually likely to decompose, while shark teeth are not. Or, the explanation could be some combination of hardy shark teeth and weak shark skeletons. In any of these cases, we would probably see lots of fossilized shark teeth but few fossilized shark skeletons. Thus, the apparent paradox would be explained.

Explain, Don't Ignore

Note that the correct answer must be consistent with the mystery, rather than disputing it. For example, something like "fossilized shark teeth actually aren't that common after all" could never be the answer. The correct answer will *explain* the situation, not pretend that the situation doesn't exist.

A) This answer, if true, makes a distinction between shark skeletons (cartilage, less likely to fossilize) and other vertebrate skeletons (bony, likely to fossilize). It also says teeth are likely to fossilize. If this is true, it would help explain how we might find lots of fossilized shark teeth but relatively few fossilized shark skeletons. This is a damn good answer, but let's see what else we've got to make sure.
B) If this is true, it doesn't explain anything. In fact, it can only make the mystery worse. Why would the skeletons (which are rare) be found in different areas from the fossilized shark teeth? Our initial question remains: Why are shark skeletons rare but teeth common? Since we can't answer this question, we haven't found the correct answer.
C) Again, if this is true, it doesn't answer our question. Why are there so many shark teeth, but so few skeletons? The correct answer should offer as clear as possible an answer to this question. This answer choice doesn't do it.
D) This is a pretty good answer. If sharks grow and lose many sets of teeth, then it stands to reason that we'd find more teeth than skeletons. If answer A didn't ex-

ist, then D would be my answer. But there are a couple problems with D. First, it says "some" species of sharks grow and lose many sets of teeth. "Some" means one or more. If there is only one species of shark that grows and loses many sets of teeth, and there are (possibly) thousands of species of sharks, then this would become a very weak explanation. It's not a fatal flaw, but it gives me a hint that this might not be the correct answer. The second problem with D is that it talks about species "that are alive today." Fossilization is probably a process that takes a long time, such that species that are alive today don't leave fossils that we find today. So sharks today that grow and lose a lot of teeth don't do a terrific job explaining why we're finding so many shark teeth from sharks that lived well before today. Again, this is a small thing. But taken together, these two issues make D a weak answer. Thankfully A is a good explanation of the paradox, so we can avoid choosing D.

E) This could only make the paradox worse. If the physical and chemical processes of shark teeth and shark skeleton fossilization are the same, why do we find more teeth than skeletons? It ain't this one. Our answer is A.

QUESTION 13:

13

Critic: Photographers, by deciding which subjects to depict and how to depict them, express their own worldviews in their photographs, however realistically those photographs may represent reality. Thus, photographs are interpretations of reality.

The argument's conclusion is properly drawn if which one of the following is assumed?

A) Even representing a subject realistically can involve interpreting that subject.
B) To express a worldview is to interpret reality.
C) All visual art expresses the artist's worldview.
D) Any interpretation of reality involves the expression of a worldview.
E) Nonrealistic photographs, like realistic photographs, express the worldviews of the photographers who take them.

This question asks us to identify an additional premise that, if it were true, would force the conclusion of the argument to be true. Here, the conclusion is "photographs are interpretations of reality." The word "interpretations" is not used anywhere else in the argument. In your legal writing class during your first year in law school, you'll learn that every critical component of an argument must be logically linked to the other components. The LSAT is the same. We can't conclude anything about "interpretations" if we don't have premises that include the term "interpretations" or its synonym. So before I go to the answer choices, I strongly suspect that the word "interpretations" must be in the correct answer.

The logic goes like this: Photographs express worldviews, therefore photographs interpret reality. There's a gap there, and we need to bridge that gap. The critic even acknowledges that some photographs may not be all that realistic, and claims that even those pictures interpret reality, so my advance answer is "Anything that expresses a worldview is an interpretation of reality." If that's true, then photographs ➡ express worldviews ➡ interpret reality, therefore photographs ➡ interpret reality.

A) This is kind of close, but uses the weak phrase "can involve," and therefore doesn't *force* the conclusion to be true. On sufficient-assumption questions like this I'm almost always looking for a very strongly worded answer. I don't think this is the one.
B) This exactly matches my advance answer, and if true it would force the conclusion of the argument to be true. I'm pretty sure this is it.
C) No use of "interpret," so this can't be the correct answer.
D) This gets the logic backward: interprets reality ➡ expresses worldview. If you're not paying attention, this one could look mighty appealing, but I was looking for expresses worldview ➡ interprets reality, so this isn't it.
E) No use of "interpret," so this can't be the correct answer. Our answer is B.

QUESTION 14:

Geologists recently discovered marks that closely resemble worm tracks in a piece of sandstone. These marks were made more than half a billion years earlier than the earliest known traces of multicellular animal life. Therefore, the marks are probably the traces of geological processes rather than of worms.

Which one of the following, if true, most weakens the argument?

A) It is sometimes difficult to estimate the precise age of a piece of sandstone.

B) Geological processes left a substantial variety of marks in sandstone more than half a billion years before the earliest known multicellular animal life existed.

C) There were some early life forms other than worms that are known to have left marks that are hard to distinguish from those found in the piece of sandstone.

D) At the place where the sandstone was found, the only geological processes that are likely to mark sandstone in ways that resemble worm tracks could not have occurred at the time the marks were made.

E) Most scientists knowledgeable about early animal life believe that worms are likely to have been among the earliest forms of multicellular animal life on Earth, but evidence of their earliest existence is scarce because they are composed solely of soft tissue.

This argument provides good evidence that worms couldn't have made marks in the sandstone: "The marks were made more than half a billion years before the earliest known traces of multicellular animal life." If this is true, then it's definitely hard to see how worms could have made the marks. But the conclusion of the argument goes much further, saying "geological processes" must have made the marks. No evidence whatsoever is provided for geological processes' ability to make the marks, making it wholly unsupported. We are asked to weaken this asserted cause-and-effect relationship.

If you need to refresh your memory, take a quick look back at the process we laid out on Question 11 on weakening a cause-and-effect question. When you're ready, let's go. Remember, incorrect answers will either strengthen the argument or be irrelevant.

A) The word "sometimes" is a clue that this is a weak answer choice, and this question type tends to prefer strong answers. Furthermore, the premises state as fact that the marks were made more than half a billion years earlier than the earliest known traces of multicellular animal life. The premises must be taken as fact, so we are not allowed to question this piece of information. If we must take as fact that the marks were made half a billion years before any traces of multicellular life, then it really doesn't matter how old the sandstone is. A, therefore, isn't the answer.

B) This, if true, would *strengthen* the argument that geological processes could have made the tracks. We're looking for a weakener, so this can be eliminated.

C) This is a strange answer. At first, I thought it could be a weakener because it's a potential alternate cause. We know the worms couldn't have done it because worms are multicellular and the marks were made before the advent of multicellular life. However, it's weakly stated in that it doesn't prove the marks were made by "other" life forms, it only suggests that it's possible. Because I'd prefer an answer that is strongly stated, I'm already skeptical. Furthermore, C doesn't say that these "other" life forms weren't themselves multicellular. If they were multicellular, then they'd be eliminated just like worms. So I doubt this can be the answer.

Only the Strong Survive

Imagine yourself as a defense attorney in a courtroom trying to blow a hole in the prosecution's murder case. Would you rather be able to argue that the defendant, your client, "sometimes" bowls on Tuesday nights? Or would you rather have a security camera tape *proving* that your client was at the bowling alley at the precise time of the murder and couldn't possibly have committed the crime? Hopefully you'd prefer the latter. (Otherwise, maybe now's the time to take a step back from this whole law school idea.) The LSAT is no different: When attacking an argument (or strengthening an argument), you'd rather have a strong piece of evidence than a weak one.

D) This answer choice says that the *only* geological processes likely to mark sandstone in this way *could not* have happened in this case. This seems to eliminate geological processes as a possible cause of the marks. It's strongly stated and it weakens the argument. It's probably going to be the best choice.

E) This answer suggests that the earliest evidence of multicellular life might not accurately account for worms because they are soft-bodied. But it doesn't prove that worms actually did exist when the marks were made. "Most scientists" think worms might have been around sometime before the evidence proves they were around, but this isn't strong enough. A much better answer would be something like "*all* scientists agree that worms existed *more than half a billion years before* the earliest known traces of multicellular animal life." This isn't what E says, so E isn't our answer. Our answer is D.

QUESTION 15:

15

Often a type of organ or body structure is the only physically feasible means of accomplishing a given task, so it should be unsurprising if, like eyes or wings, that type of organ or body structure evolves at different times in a number of completely unrelated species. After all, whatever the difference of heritage and habitat, as organisms animals have fundamentally similar needs and so _____.

Which one of the following most logically completes the last sentence of the passage?

A) will often live in the same environment as other species quite different from themselves
B) will in many instances evolve similar adaptations enabling them to satisfy these needs
C) will develop adaptations allowing them to satisfy these needs
D) will resemble other species having different biological needs
E) will all develop eyes or wings as adaptations

This question tests our ability to follow along with the logic of an argument and predict where it is likely to go. Since the completion has to be "logical," whatever answer we pick has to be supported by the evidence already in the passage.

Here, the argument says it "should be unsurprising" if the same organ or body structure evolves separately in more than one species if that organ or body structure is the only feasible means to accomplish a certain task. Eyes and wings are given as two examples. The final line of the argument says "animals have fundamentally similar needs and so _____." We are asked to complete the argument. Having an advance answer at the ready is key here. If you were following along, hopefully you said something like "they'll evolve similar organs or body structures." This would logically complete the last sentence of the passage.

A) "Live in the same environment" is not what I was looking for. Next!
B) "Similar adaptations" is very close to my advance answer. I notice that it uses the qualifier "in many instances," which matches the relatively weak language of "should be unsurprising" given in the passage. This is probably the answer.
C) This sounds good at first blush, but it says nothing about "similar" adaptations, so this probably isn't the answer. Another hint: It says "*will* develop adaptations" without any sort of qualifier. This sounds too absolute to me, given the weak language in the argument.
D) "Resembling" other species is not necessarily the same thing has having similar adaptations. Not close enough.
E) Animals have similar needs, therefore they'll evolve eyes or wings specifically? This answer sticks far too closely to specifics and misses the broader point of the argument. Our answer is B.

Efficient Guessing

After much practice, you'll learn whether or not you're likely to finish the sections in time. (Most students don't.) So you're probably going to be doing some guessing. It's critical that you get something bubbled in for every question before time is called, even if it's a complete guess—there's no penalty for wrong answers.

The best strategy I've heard for guessing is very simple. At the five-minute warning, go ahead and bubble in a guess for any question you haven't yet answered. This should only take 20 seconds or so. Then resume answering the questions like normal, erasing your guesses and bubbling in new answers as you go. This way, when time is called, you can put your pencil down immediately, confident that you're not leaving any potential points on the table.

16

QUESTION 16:

Engineer: Thermophotovoltaic generators are devices that convert heat into electricity. The process of manufacturing steel produces huge amounts of heat that currently go to waste. So if steel-manufacturing plants could feed the heat they produce into thermophotovoltaic generators, they would greatly reduce their electric bills, thereby saving money.

Which one of the following is an assumption on which the engineer's argument depends?

A) There is no other means of utilizing the heat produced by the steel-manufacturing process that would be more cost effective than installing thermophotovoltaic generators.
B) Using current technology, it would be possible for steel-manufacturing plants to feed the heat they produce into thermophotovoltaic generators in such a way that those generators could convert at least some of that heat into electricity.
C) The amount steel-manufacturing plants would save on their electric bills by feeding heat into thermophotovoltaic generators would be sufficient to cover the cost of purchasing and installing those generators.
D) At least some steel-manufacturing plants rely on electricity as their primary source of energy in the steel-manufacturing process.
E) There are at least some steel-manufacturing plants that could greatly reduce their electricity bills only if they used some method of converting wasted heat or other energy from the steel-manufacturing process into electricity.

Contrast the language of this question with that of Question 13. In 13, a sufficient-assumption question, we were asked to identify a premise that, if added to the argument, would be sufficient information to prove the argument's conclusion. Here, we're doing something a little different.

Necessary-assumption questions ask us to identify an assumption that the author has already made, *i.e.*, to identify something that is *necessary* in order for his argument to be valid. If the argument depends on something, we're looking for something that *must be true* in order for the argument to make sense. In other words, we're looking for something that, *if not true*, causes the argument to fall apart at the seams.

It's helpful on all assumption questions (and, really, on all Logical Reasoning questions) to focus tightly on the conclusion of the argument. Here, the conclusion is conditional (it uses an if → then statement). According to the argument, if steel-manufacturing plants could feed the heat they produce into thermophotovoltaic generators, two things would happen. First, they would greatly reduce their electric bills. Second, they would save money. Since I'm looking for a necessary assumption, I'm looking for a missing premise of the argument. In other words, I'm looking for something that must be true, or else one or both parts of the conclusion will fail.

A) It's irrelevant whether there are other means of utilizing the heat. Steel manufacturers don't necessarily have to have used the very best method of saving energy and money in order to, in line with the argument's prediction, have saved on their energy bills and saved money. The author has not assumed that this is the best method, only that this particular method will work.
B) The author has not necessarily assumed that it's actually possible, using "current" technology, to carry out his proposal. He has qualified his conclusion by saying "if" it were possible, steel manufacturers would save money. No dice.
C) Because the author predicts manufacturers will not only save on their energy bills, but thereby save money overall, he has necessarily assumed that the energy savings would outweigh the cost of the thermophotovoltaic generators. If C is not true, then the manufacturers would not save money overall. Because C must be true in order for the entire conclusion of the argument to be true, the argument "depends" on C. This is a necessary assumption—and probably the correct answer.
D) It is true that at least some manufacturers must use electricity in some manner, or the argument would fail, because otherwise how would they save on their "electricity" bills? But this answer choice goes too far by using the phrase "primary

source." Electricity can still be costly without being a primary source of energy. The author has not assumed that electricity is a primary source of energy for any manufacturer. It would still be possible for manufacturers to save on their energy bills, and save money overall, even if electricity were a secondary, tertiary, or even lower-importance source of energy. D is not required in order for the conclusion to make sense, so it isn't the answer for a necessary assumption.

E) The author never claims (or implies) that converting wasted heat into electricity would be the *only* method for reducing electricity bills for any manufacturer. Note how similar E is to A. A tried to trap us into believing that the author said his method is the *best* method, while E tries to trap us into believing that the author said his method is the *only* method for some manufacturers. The argument made neither of these claims, so A and E are both wrong. Our answer is C.

QUESTION 17:

Herbalist: While standard antibiotics typically have just one active ingredient, herbal antibacterial remedies typically contain several. Thus, such herbal remedies are more likely to retain their effectiveness against new, resistant strains of bacteria than are standard antibiotics. For a strain of bacteria, the difficulty of developing resistance to an herbal antibacterial remedy is like a cook's difficulty in trying to prepare a single meal that will please all of several dozen guests, a task far more difficult than preparing one meal that will please a single guest.

In the analogy drawn in the argument above, which one of the following corresponds to a standard antibiotic?

A) a single guest
B) several dozen guests
C) the pleasure experienced by a single guest
D) a cook
E) the ingredients available to a cook

This is a unique question, and doesn't fit into any of the major categories of question types. This might have made me uncomfortable if I had read the question before the argument. But hopefully you're not in the habit of doing that, because it's almost never advantageous to do so. Use the same general technique on every question: Read the argument closely and look for weaknesses. Then, having understood the argument as best you can, read the question.

Here, the herbalist is arguing that herbal antibacterial remedies are better than standard antibiotics. To do so, she uses an analogy that compares bacteria to cooks. Cooks, she says, have a harder time pleasing several guests than they do just one guest. If a bacterium is a cook, then it will have a much harder time "pleasing" (*i.e.*, avoiding) an antibacterial remedy with several "guests" (*i.e.*, active ingredients) than an antibiotic with just one active ingredient.

Frankly, I think the argument sucks. It's a nifty analogy I suppose, both novel and interesting, but it has one huge problem: What on earth do antibiotics have to do with cooking? The answer is, of course, nothing, therefore the argument is extremely weak. (A more appropriate analogy might have been something like "the human body is most effective when it uses several different agents to combat an invader, therefore an antibacterial remedy should also contain several active agents.")

Okay, so I've understood the argument. Now I'll read the question, which asks me to identify which part of the analogy represents a standard antibiotic. The answer, of course, is one guest. The herbalist says her herbal antibacterial remedy is like a crowd of guests, which no bacterial chef can possibly please all at once, while a standard antibiotic is like a single guest, easily pleased by a chef. Note that I'm no longer concerned with whether the analogy actually applies. I've put my criticism aside and I'm simply answering the question. Coming up with an advance answer is really the only way to answer this question. Either you've got it or you don't. No lengthy analysis of the answer choices is likely to help you here.

David Cross: Attorney at Law

As comedian David Cross noted, people who support the three-strikes rule for lifetime imprisonment of thrice-convicted felons seem to believe that the policy is a good idea because "It's like baseball!" But unless criminal justice has some important common thread with the game of baseball in the first place, then using the game to justify the policy is purely nonsensical. Beware of nifty-sounding analogies that lack a practical connection to the matter at hand.

A) A single guest, this exactly matches my advance answer. I'm tempted to just bubble it and move on because I'm tired of thinking about bacterial chefs (gross), but let's see what else we've got just to make sure.
B) Not several dozen guests, one single guest.
C) Not "the pleasure" experienced by a guest.
D) Not a cook.
E) Not the ingredients. Our answer is A.

QUESTION 18:

To find out how barn owls learn how to determine the direction from which sounds originate, scientists put distorting lenses over the eyes of young barn owls before the owls first opened their eyes. The owls with these lenses behaved as if objects making sounds were farther to the right than they actually were. Once the owls matured, the lenses were removed, yet the owls continued to act as if they misjudged the location of the source of sounds. The scientists consequently hypothesized that once a barn owl has developed an auditory scheme for estimating the point from which sounds originate, it ceases to use vision to locate sounds.

The scientists' reasoning is vulnerable to which one of the following criticisms?

A) It fails to consider whether the owls' vision was permanently impaired by their having worn the lenses while immature.
B) It assumes that the sense of sight is equally good in all owls.
C) It attributes human reasoning processes to a nonhuman organism.
D) It neglects to consider how similar distorting lenses might affect the behavior of other bird species.
E) It uses as evidence experimental results that were irrelevant to the conclusion.

This argument is about a horrifically inhumane study on barn owls. Scientists put distorting lenses on the eyes of baby barn owls, which caused the owls to look for sounds farther to the right of where they actually were. They removed the lenses once the owls matured, and the owls continued to look for sounds farther to the right of where they actually were. From this, the scientists reach the puzzling hypothesis that all owls, once they've developed an auditory scheme for estimating the point from which sounds originate, "cease to use vision" to locate sounds.

This is a cause-and-effect hypothesis. Why did the owls in the study continue to look too far to the right? The scientists think the cause is that the owls are no longer using vision. But they're ignoring the elephant in the room: These owls could have been permanently effed up by the scientists' jerkface experiment—and that would be a much simpler explanation!

A) Exactly. If it's true that the owls were permanently damaged by the experiment, then the scientists cannot possibly conclude that owls "cease to use vision." The experiment is invalid because the test subjects were ruined by the experiment.
B) The argument never assumes that the sense of sight is "equally good" in all owls, and even if it did, A still points out a much bigger flaw.
C) The argument never attributes human reasoning to animals.
D) This is true but it is not a flaw. Other bird species aren't relevant to the scientists' hypothesis about owls, so they're permitted to "neglect" other bird species.
E) The evidence (an experiment about auditory processing in owls) was not "irrelevant" to the conclusion (about the auditory processing of owls). The study was flawed, but it was not irrelevant. Evidence is only "irrelevant" when it is completely off topic. Our answer is A.

QUESTION 19:

As often now as in the past, newspaper journalists use direct or indirect quotation to report unsupported or false claims made by newsmakers. However, journalists are becoming less likely to openly challenge the veracity of such claims within their articles.

Each of the following, if true, helps to explain the trend in journalism described above EXCEPT:

A) Newspaper publishers have found that many readers will cancel a subscription simply because a view they take for granted has been disputed by the publication.
B) The areas of knowledge on which journalists report are growing in specialization and diversity, while journalists themselves are not becoming more broadly knowledgeable.
C) Persons supporting controversial views more and more frequently choose to speak only to reporters who seem sympathetic to their views.
D) A basic principle of journalism holds that debate over controversial issues draws the attention of the public.
E) Journalists who challenge the veracity of claims are often criticized for failing their professional obligation to be objective.

The first thing I note when I turn to this page is that there are only three questions on the page instead of four. This is because the questions tend to get longer and harder as the sections progress. Obviously, the best case is that you can answer every question in the section correctly. But if you're ever going to guess, you should be guessing on these later questions and not the earlier, more manageable ones.

This question states that journalists are becoming less likely to openly challenge unsupported or false claims made by newsmakers, then asks us to identify reasons for this phenomenon. In other words, why is this happening? Because it is an EXCEPT question, four incorrect answers will provide satisfying answers to this question. The correct answer will not provide a satisfying explanation.

A) If publishers are worried about cancellations that occur when certain ideas are challenged, it's not a far stretch to imagine that they might pressure their journalists not to challenge those ideas. This is a good explanation, so it's not the answer.
B) If journalists are writing on areas of specialization that they're not actually knowledgeable about, then they probably won't challenge the ideas they encounter in their reporting. Another good explanation.
C) If people espousing controversial views only give interviews to people that agree with them (think cable news shows), then their ideas probably won't get challenged. This is another good explanation, so it's not the answer either.
D) If the public likes controversy, wouldn't journalists provide it? D doesn't give a satisfying explanation (in fact, it only makes me scratch my head more), so it's got to be the correct answer to this "explain... EXCEPT" question.
E) If journalists get criticized for challenging claims, they might eventually stop challenging claims. This is yet another good explanation. Our answer is D.

QUESTION 20:

When people show signs of having a heart attack an electrocardiograph (EKG) is often used to diagnose their condition. In a study, a computer program for EKG diagnosis of heart attacks was pitted against a very experienced, highly skilled cardiologist. The program correctly diagnosed a significantly higher proportion of the cases that were later confirmed to be heart attacks than did the cardiologist. Interpreting EKG data, therefore, should be left to computer programs.

Which one of the following, if true, most weakens the argument?

A) Experts agreed that the cardiologist made few obvious mistakes in

reading and interpreting the EKG data.
B) The practice of medicine is as much an art as a science, and computer programs are not easily adapted to making subjective judgments.
C) The cardiologist correctly diagnosed a significantly higher proportion of the cases in which no heart attack occurred than did the computer program.
D) In a considerable percentage of cases, EKG data alone are insufficient to enable either computer programs or cardiologists to make accurate diagnoses.
E) The cardiologist in the study was unrepresentative of cardiologists in general with respect to skill and experience.

This argument discusses a study that compares the success rates of a computer program and a cardiologist in evaluating EKG results to assess whether or not a patient had a heart attack. The computer program, according to the study, correctly diagnosed a higher proportion of cases that were later confirmed to be heart attacks than did the cardiologist. Therefore, according to the argument, EKG analysis should always be performed by computer.

The argument makes a very simple mistake, however. It's focused only on cases that were later confirmed to be actual heart attacks, and has completely ignored all the cases that were later deemed not to have been heart attacks. Consider what would have happened in this study if I had trained a monkey to hold up a sign that says "Yes indeed, this EKG shows that a heart attack has most certainly occurred" every single time an EKG is presented. If I had done this, then my monkey would have been correct in 100% of cases that were later confirmed to be heart attacks! Following the same logic, the author would have to conclude that EKG analysis should be performed by trained monkeys. And I have to admit that I don't think I'd be completely comfortable with that.

It's useful to think about four types of results in a case like this:

1) True positives: There was a heart attack, and it was correctly diagnosed by the EKG interpreter.
2) False positives: There was not a heart attack, but the EKG interpreter falsely concluded there was.
3) True negatives: There was not a heart attack, and the EKG interpreter correctly concluded that there was not.
4) False negatives: There was a heart attack, but the EKG interpreter falsely concluded there was not.

The stakes can be very high when evaluating these types of tests, and it is useful to think about which type of error is more dangerous. Think about a DNA test in a murder trial. A false negative might let a murderer walk free, which is certainly bad. But a false positive might send a perfectly innocent man to prison for life, which most of us would conclude is even worse.

My advance answer on this question is something like "What about the false positives? If the cardiologist had far fewer false positives, then she could still be better at evaluating EKGs than the computer program, even if the computer program had fewer false negatives."

A) I'm not sure whether it would be good or bad for the cardiologist to make "few" obvious mistakes. Certainly it's better than "many" obvious mistakes, but then again, what if the computer program made "zero" obvious mistakes? Because I can see how this answer could both strengthen and weaken the argument, I don't think it's the correct answer.
B) This seems to argue against the conclusion that EKGs should be analyzed by computer, but it does nothing to counter the evidence that the EKG actually did provide a more accurate analysis of the true positives. Because it doesn't use the evidence and attack the analysis of the argument, I doubt it's the correct answer.
C) This matches my advance answer. It says that the cardiologist had fewer false positives, and is therefore the front-runner.
D) Who cares if in some cases (even if it's a "considerable percentage" of cases) EKG data alone is insufficient? The argument never says that EKG data "alone" should be used to make diagnoses. The argument is solely about whether a computer or a cardiologist is better at evaluating EKG data. Even if D is true, it does nothing to weaken the case for the computer, so it's not the answer.
E) If this is true, it can only strengthen the case for the computer. The cardiologist here was "very experienced" and "highly skilled." If other cardiologists were less experienced and skilled, then the computer would seem an even better choice. This isn't the answer if I'm looking for a weakener. Our answer is C.

21

QUESTION 21:

A government study indicates that raising speed limits to reflect the actual average speeds of traffic on level, straight stretches of high-speed roadways reduces the accident rate. Since the actual average speed for level, straight stretches of high-speed roadways tends to be 120 kilometers per hour (75 miles per hour), that should be set as a uniform national speed limit for level, straight stretches of all such roadways.

Which one of the following principles, if valid, most helps to justify the reasoning above?

A) Uniform national speed limits should apply only to high-speed roadways.
B) Traffic laws applying to high-speed roadways should apply uniformly across the nation.
C) A uniform national speed limit for high-speed roadways should be set only if all such roadways have roughly equal average speeds of traffic.
D) Long-standing laws that are widely violated are probably not good laws.
E) Any measure that reduces the rate of traffic accidents should be implemented.

The use of the word "most" in the question indicates that this is not a sufficient-assumption question, but simply a "strengthen" question. (The correct answer need not actually prove the conclusion, but will strengthen the conclusion in some way.) The argument starts with a premise, describing a study that indicates that raising speed limits to "the actual average speeds of traffic" on level, straight stretches of high-speed roadways reduces accidents. Then the argument gives another premise, that 75 miles per hour is the actual average speed for such roadways. Finally, the argument concludes that 75 miles per hour *should* be set as the national speed limit for all such roadways.

The use of the word "should" is always a red flag for me. Why "should" we make this change? The obvious answer is "to reduce accidents" but there is no premise in the argument that says "we should reduce accidents." While I'm sure that no one would disagree with fewer accidents being a good thing, please remember that nothing can be taken for granted on the LSAT or, more broadly, in legal writing. Without a piece of evidence that says we "should" reduce accidents, it cannot be assumed that reducing accidents is our priority. Perhaps there are other factors that need to be considered. What about fuel efficiency? What about pollution? Perhaps a lower speed limit would be better for energy consumption and the environment. If this were true, would it still be true that we "should" raise the speed limit to reduce accidents? To strengthen the argument, I'm looking to plug the gap in the argument with something like "we should reduce the accident rate," because that's what ties those thoughts together.

A) The word "should" is present, but nothing about the accident rate.
B) Again, the word "should" is present, but nothing about the accident rate.
C) Lots of "should," but nothing about the accident rate, and also there's a weird usage of "only if" which doesn't seem like a very strong strengthener.
D) No use of "should," so this is very unlikely to be the answer here.
E) This matches nicely with my advance answer, and I love how strongly the answer choice is worded: "*Any* measure... should be implemented." When I'm trying to strengthen an argument, I want a strong piece of additional information. This is our answer.

22

QUESTION 22:

Psychiatrist: In treating first-year students at this university, I have noticed that those reporting the highest levels of spending on recreation score at about the same level on standard screening instruments for anxiety and depression as those reporting the lowest levels of spending on recreation. This suggests that the first-year students with high levels of spending on recreation could reduce that spending without increasing their anxiety or depression.

Each of the following, if true, strengthens the psychiatrist's argument EXCEPT:

A) At other universities, first-year students reporting the highest levels of spending on recreation also show the same degree of anxiety and depression as do those reporting the lowest levels of such spending.

B) Screening of first-year students at the university who report moderate levels of spending on recreation reveals that those students are less anxious and depressed than both those with the highest and those with the lowest levels of spending on recreation.

C) Among adults between the ages of 40 and 60, increased levels of spending on recreation are strongly correlated with decreased levels of anxiety and depression.

D) The screening instruments used by the psychiatrist are extremely accurate in revealing levels of anxiety and depression among university students.

E) Several of the psychiatrist's patients who are first-year students at the university have reduced their spending on recreation from very high levels to very low levels without increasing their anxiety or depression.

Do enough practicing for the LSAT, and you'll start to see errant correlation-equals-causation arguments a mile away. This is one of them. The argument starts off with a correlation (actually, a lack of a correlation) between 1) the amount of money spent on recreation and 2) anxiety and depression. The argument then suggests that, because there is no apparent correlation between the two variables, there isn't a *causal* relationship either. At least this would seem to be the assumption, given the recommendation that the high-spending students could reduce their spending on recreation without increasing their anxiety or depression.

My immediate objection to this line of reasoning was "No, what if the students who spent more money on recreation needed to do so just to maintain an average level of anxiety and depression? What if they were anxious/depressed before they bought their gym memberships, and are now back to normal levels?" In other words, the psychiatrist's only evidence is an observed correlation, with no causal evidence whatsoever. Here's another example that might make the logic more clear: "Men with hair plugs appear to have just as much hair as do men with natural hair. Therefore, men with hair plugs could remove their plugs and still appear to have as much hair as do men with natural hair." Sounds crazy now, right?

Because this is an EXCEPT question, four incorrect answers will strengthen the argument and the correct answer will either weaken the argument or be irrelevant.

A) This strengthens because it shows that the correlation that the psychiatrist observed is not an anomaly that can only be observed here, but also holds at other universities. Note that this isn't a great strengthener, because it says nothing about causation. But because the psychiatrist would prefer that it is true than not true, it strengthens his argument slightly.

B) This is a strengthener because it provides some data about the middle of the range, whereas the psychiatrist's initial observations were only about the top and bottom of the range. This, like A, goes toward strengthening the correlation that has been observed. Again, there's still nothing about causation so it's not a terrific strengthener, but it's enough to knock B out of contention here.

C) This is off target, because it's about the wrong age group. Furthermore, even if it were about college students, it would only weaken the observed correlation. This is a good answer to an EXCEPT question, and it's the leader so far.

D) There's nothing about causation so it's not a perfect strengthener, but it does reinforce the argument by showing that the psychiatric evaluations are accurate. It's not what we're looking for.

E) This is the best strengthener, because it shows people have actually made the change the psychiatrist is suggesting, and experienced the same predicted effect. It's a great trap if you glaze over the question, because this is what I would choose if I had accidentally ignored the "EXCEPT." Our answer is C.

23

QUESTION 23:

Every brick house on River Street has a front yard. Most of the houses on River Street that have front yards also have two stories. So most of the brick houses on River Street have two stories.

Which one of the following is most appropriate as an analogy demonstrating that the reasoning in the argument above is flawed?

A) By that line of reasoning, we could conclude that most politicians have run for office, since all legislators are politicians and most legislators have run for office.

B) By that line of reasoning, we could conclude that most public servants are legislators, since most legislators have run for office and most politicians who have run for office are public servants.

C) By that line of reasoning, we could conclude that not every public servant has run for office, since every legislator is a public servant but some public servants are not legislators.

D) By that line of reasoning, we could conclude that most legislators have never run for office, since most public servants have never run for office and all legislators are public servants.

E) By that line of reasoning, we could conclude that most legislators are not public servants, since most public servants have not run for office and most legislators have run for office.

Ugh. This question just plain sucks. It's abstract, it's highly technical, and most students should probably skip it. Seriously. This question is the difference between a 175 and a 176 on the test. If you're nowhere near that level yet, then there's plenty more lower-hanging fruit that you could be harvesting.

Still here? Okay, well, the flaw is actually somewhat commonly tested on the LSAT. But it's given in a completely abstract way. (River Street? Arbitrary rules about brick houses, front yards, and two stories? This might as well be Greek.)

Maybe I can demonstrate the flaw with a concrete example. Consider this logic: Everyone on the San Francisco Giants is a Major League Baseball player. Most Major League Baseball players don't play their home games at San Francisco's AT&T Park. Therefore most San Francisco Giants don't play their home games at AT&T Park.

Bonkers, right? Of course "most" of the Giants play their home games at AT&T Park. In fact, they all do!

We're looking for a similar flawed line of reasoning. Hopefully, we'll find an answer choice that is obviously nonsensical in the exact same way as my Giants example.

A) Or, not. Scanning down the list, I see that all the answer choices contain arbitrary rules about legislators, politicians, and who has run for office and who has not. So these answer choices also may as well be in Greek. We're not going to find an answer choice that jumps out at us in the way my Giants example did. Instead, we're going to have to get super-technical, and answer the question in a very abstract way. The logic we're looking for is "All X are Y, and most Y are Z, therefore most X are Z." That's flawed because there could be a million OTHER people in the Y group that were not included in the original X group. (Applying this to my Giants example, there are a lot of other people in MLB besides the San Francisco Giants.) Answer A doesn't follow this pattern, unfortunately. A says "All X (legislators) are Y (politicians), and most X (legislators) are Z (have run for office), therefore most Y (politicians) are Z (have run for office)." I think that's flawed, but in a slightly different way. Super-tough question here. I told you to skip it!

B) Here, there are two "mosts," which doesn't match the argument we were presented. It's easier to get past this answer than it was to get past A.

C) Now we have a "not" and a "some," neither of which match the argument. No way.

D) Aha! This answer follows the "All X (legislators) are Y (public servants), and most Y (public servants) are Z (have never run for office), therefore most X (legislators) are Z (have never run for office)" pattern. That's a better match than A, so it's the best answer so far.

E) Too many "mosts" without an "all." This doesn't match, so our answer is D.

QUESTION 24:

Historian: It is unlikely that someone would see history as the working out of moral themes unless he or she held clear and unambiguous moral beliefs. However, one's inclination to morally judge human behavior decreases as one's knowledge of history increases. Consequently, the more history a person knows, the less likely that person is to view history as the working out of moral themes.

The conclusion of the argument is properly drawn if which one of the following is assumed?

A) Historical events that fail to elicit moral disapproval are generally not considered to exemplify a moral theme.

B) The less inclined one is to morally judge human behavior, the less likely it is that one holds clear and unambiguous moral beliefs.

C) Only those who do not understand human history attribute moral significance to historical events.

D) The more clear and unambiguous one's moral beliefs, the more likely one is to view history as the working out of moral themes.

E) People tend to be less objective regarding a subject about which they possess extensive knowledge than regarding a subject about which they do not possess extensive knowledge.

I don't diagram for Logical Reasoning unless I'm in trouble. I'll only diagram if I feel that I absolutely have to, which usually happens once or twice per section. So far I haven't diagrammed a single question, but here I had no choice. Diagramming can be helpful, but it's very time consuming. Also, it usually adds a level of abstraction that can sometimes be confusing—but on certain questions it can make everything much more clear.

I diagrammed the first sentence of the premise as "~CUMB → WMT less likely." (If you don't have clear and unambiguous moral beliefs, it is less likely that you will view history as the working out of moral themes.) I diagrammed the second sentence as "H increases → MJHB decreases." (As knowledge of history increases, one's inclination to morally judge human behavior decreases.) The conclusion of the argument I diagrammed as "H increases → WMT less likely."

Since this is a sufficient-assumption question, our job is to identify a premise that, when added to the existing premises, makes the conclusion logically valid. There can't be any holes when we are done. It all has to be tight, with no missing pieces.

I rearranged the diagrams to get "H increases → *MJHB decreases* → ~CUMB → WMT less likely." The italicized part didn't exist in the argument as presented, but if it is true, it will make the argument logically sound. This was my advance answer, and the correct answer will likely be some variation of this.

A) This doesn't contain ~CUMB, therefore I can't see how it can be the answer.

B) This almost exactly matches my advance answer. I can't see what else we could hope for, but let's make sure.

C) This doesn't have MJHB or ~CUMB.

D) This doesn't have MJHB.

E) This doesn't have MJHB or ~CUMB. Our answer is B.

25

QUESTION 25:

A recent poll revealed that most students at our university prefer that the university, which is searching for a new president, hire someone who has extensive experience as a university president. However, in the very same poll, the person most students chose from among a list of leading candidates as the one they would most like to see hired was someone who has never served as a university president.

Which one of the following, if true, most helps to account for the apparent discrepancy in the students' preferences?

A) Because several of the candidates listed in the poll had extensive experience as university presidents, not all of the candidates could be differentiated on this basis alone.
B) Most of the candidates listed in the poll had extensive experience as university presidents.
C) Students taking the poll had fewer candidates to choose from than were currently being considered for the position.
D) Most of the students taking the poll did not know whether any of the leading candidates listed in the poll had ever served as a university president.
E) Often a person can be well suited to a position even though they have relatively little experience in such a position.

It's critical on "explain" questions that we know what we're trying to explain. Usually this is some sort of puzzling situation. It's extremely important that before going to the answer choices, we articulate what the problem is. (If you're not sure what the problem is, the answer choices are only going to confuse you more.) Here, the puzzling situation is "Why did the students say they wanted an experienced president, yet actually picked someone from the list who had no experience at all?"

There could be several possible explanations. Maybe nobody on the list had any experience, so the students had no choice but to pick someone inexperienced. Maybe experience is not these students' only priority, but one of many. If either of these were true, it could explain how students could say one thing, but then (apparently) do another. The correct answer could be one of these explanations, or could be a different explanation entirely. The important thing is that the correct answer will make the puzzling info make sense.

A) If there were lots of experienced candidates on the list, then why on earth would the students choose someone inexperienced? This doesn't explain the mystery to me, so it's not my answer.
B) Same as A.
C) This doesn't explain anything. Even if the students couldn't see all the candidates on their list, why would they choose someone inexperienced?
D) This makes some sense. If the students didn't know they were choosing someone inexperienced, then it's not incongruous for them to say they want experience and choose someone inexperienced. Sounds good.
E) This is probably true, but doesn't help to explain why the students said one thing and did another. It's out. Our answer is D.

SECTION
THREE

Analytical Reasoning (Logic Games)

(Or: Shit You Know For Sure)

On games, just like the rest of the LSAT, you have to slow down in order to speed up. First, the good news: Hardly anybody completes all four games. So our goal here is to slow down and focus on accuracy.

Unlike the rest of the LSAT, where often you have to pick the best of a bad bunch of answers, every question on the logic games has a single, objectively correct answer. There is no picking the "best" answer on the logic games. Rather, there are four terrible answers that you hate and one perfect answer that you love. Focus on answering the questions with 100% certainty. For starters, see if you can just get every answer right on a single game. If you can do this in 35 minutes, you're on the right track. Next, see if you can do two games perfectly in 35 minutes. Believe it or not, that would put you well ahead of the average test taker. If you can do three games perfectly, you'll be in the top 90 percent. But you have to walk before you can run.

My general process for Logic Games is as follows:

1. **Read through the entire scenario and all of the rules before doing anything else.** That lets you get the lay of the land before you start messing up the page. Remember that there is no scratch paper allowed, so have a sharp pencil, write small, and think before you write.

2. **Take enough time to understand exactly what each rule means.** Sometimes a single rule will have three pieces of information in it. For example, a rule might say "B must go before A and after C, but can't go fourth." There are really three rules here. (1. B before A; 2. B after C; 3. B can't go fourth.) If you miss any one of these rules, you'll struggle with the game. Conversely, sometimes a rule will mean *less* than you think it means at first blush. For example, the rule might say "A, B, C, D, and E are available for interviews." This does NOT mean that each of these people must interview! Look for another rule that says "Each candidate must interview exactly once," or "there will be five interviews and no candidate can interview twice." If these rules are not present, then it's possible that one or

more of the candidates might not interview at all, and/or one or more candidates might interview more than once. The slightest mistake can ruin the entire game, so read carefully, and absolutely do not rush.

3. **Make a diagram that incorporates as much information about the game as possible.** Sometimes, this will be a diagram that is exactly like something you've seen on a previous game. Frequently, you'll be able to use a diagram similar to a game you've seen before, but you'll have to make some minor tweaks. Occasionally, you'll have to invent something entirely new. But never fear: You'll be equipped to do this once you've practiced these methods.

4. **As you diagram, take the time to consider the rules not only alone, but also in the context of the other rules.** The big prep companies will call this "making inferences" as if it's some kind of magical process. But all we're really doing is writing down shit we know for sure. Usually, the first "inferences" come from simply combining two rules together. For example, if A comes before B and there are only seven spots, then A can't go last, because there would be no room left for B. This isn't rocket science. (Hey, B can't go first either, because where would A go?! I'm a genius.) Any time you learn something for sure, no matter how small, write it down. Like a porta-potty at a rock concert, little things will add up fast.

5. **Remember that more powerful inferences come from combining three rules together, or from combining a rule with an inference, or from combining two inferences together.** Every time you make a new inference, you get to consider that inference in light of everything else you know about the game, and frequently you'll be able to make *another* inference. (Which might lead to another, and another...) Don't short-circuit this process by going to the questions too soon. Always remember that the questions are designed to confuse you! It's much better to invest the time up front in a solid solution rather than frantically trying to answer the questions without having a good foundation. Some of what you're writing down at this stage will directly answer some of the questions you'll see later.

Be a Pencil Pusher

Don't be afraid to take action. Each mark you make won't be an earth-shattering revelation, especially not at the beginning. The point is to simply start writing down the things you know for sure. Start by writing down your list of variables. Does this solve the game immediately? Of course not. But it gets you moving in the right direction, which is much better than freezing up and doing nothing at all.

6. **Move on to the questions when—and only when—you're ready.** "Okay, but how do I know when it's time to go to the questions?" Every class asks me this question, and my answer is always the same: Only you can really tell, through lots and lots of practice. The truth is that every game is different, and some games allow more inferences than others. Sometimes, I'll invest five or six minutes before going to the questions. On other games, I'll feel like I've learned all I can after a minute or two and go ahead to the questions. Personally, if I get stuck for 45-60 seconds without making any new inferences then I'm probably ready to proceed to the questions.

Solitaire Logic

Making inferences is like playing solitaire. You're only stuck in solitaire when you go through the entire deck without doing anything new. Every time you place even a single card, you get to go back through the whole deck to see what new possibilities have opened up. Tiny moves can have huge significance! Don't give up or panic too soon.

I realize this isn't a very satisfactory answer, but it's the truth. The logic games are partially art and partially science. You'll need to practice, practice, practice on the games until you get a feel for it. The payoff can be huge. I've never met a single student who couldn't eventually make a plus-5 or plus-6 question leap on the Logic Games. It's the most learnable section of the test. And it's also the most fun.

Game One

Exactly six workers—Faith, Gus, Hannah, Juan, Kenneth, and Lisa—will travel to a business convention in two cars—car 1 and car 2. Each car must carry at least two of the workers, one of whom will be assigned to drive. For the entire trip, the workers will comply with an assignment that also meets the following constraints:

Either Faith or Gus must drive the car in which Hannah travels.
Either Faith or Kenneth must drive the car in which Juan travels.
Gus must travel in the same car as Lisa.

Game One Explanation (Questions 1-5)

This game is what some would call "hybrid" in that we're not just putting things in groups or putting things in specific spots. Instead we're doing both. We have to decide who goes in what car *and* who drives each car. I've seen this sort of thing before, but there's no single template we can use that is going to provide a perfect solution. (There almost never is.) Like always, we're going to have to do some improvisation.

The first thing we learned about this game is that there are either four seats in one car and two in the other, or there are three seats in each car. We can make this inference because the scenario tells us that each car must carry at least two workers.

My suspicion is that we can make some headway by focusing on the drivers. The strongest pieces of information are the ones that are the most limiting, and here, the drivers are the most limited. I notice that there are two players (H and J) who are particular about who drives their car. I also notice that F is one of the preferred drivers of both H and J. I am guessing that if F drives, there is going to be a lot of flexibility in the rest of the setup. But if F *doesn't* drive, there are going to be some problems. If F does not drive, then H has to go in G's car, and J will require that K drives his car.

The first thing to do is pencil out a world (World 1 in the diagram below) where F doesn't drive. G will have to drive for H, and L will have to ride in this car as well because G and L travel together. F can ride in either car. This world can be either a 4-2 split or a 3-3 split. Having made this first world, we can go ahead and pencil out the other three possible driver scenarios.

World 2 is where F drives for both H and J, forcing G and L into the other car (because we can't have five people in one car). In this scenario, K can ride in either car. Any one of G, L, and K can drive their car because the people with driver restrictions have already been satisfied.

World 3 is where F drives for H but not J. In this world, J will require that K drive him in the other car. That leaves G and L, who must travel together, in either car. (So it has to be a 4-2 split in this world.)

World 4 is where F drives for J but not H. In this world, H will require that G drive him in the other car. L will have to ride in G's car. K is left over, and can ride in either car.

This might seem like a lot of work, but we've actually made things very easy for ourselves from here on out. We no longer have to remember any rules because everything's written out, and the questions should be a breeze.

REFERENCE DIAGRAMS

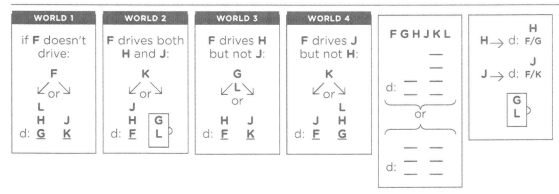

1

QUESTION 1:

Which one of the following is a possible assignment of the workers to the cars?

A) Car 1: Faith (driver), Hannah, and Juan
   Car 2: Gus (driver), Kenneth, and Lisa
B) Car 1: Faith (driver), Hannah, and Kenneth
   Car 2: Lisa (driver), Gus, and Juan
C) Car 1: Faith (driver), Juan, Kenneth, and Lisa
   Car 2: Gus (driver) and Hannah
D) Car 1: Faith (driver) and Juan
   Car 2: Kenneth (driver), Gus, Hannah, and Lisa
E) Car 1: Gus (driver), Hannah, and Lisa
   Car 2: Juan (driver), Faith, and Kenneth

This type of question is best solved by process of elimination. It's easier to eliminate the answers that must be false than positively identify the answer that could be true. We're just going to take each rule and eliminate as many answer choices as possible, and at the end, we'll be left with the correct answer.

Rule 1: H must be driven by F or G. This gets rid of answer D.
Rule 2: J must be driven by F or K. This eliminates both B and E.
Rule 3: G and L must ride together. C is gone.

Boom: Answer A has survived all of the rules, so it's our answer by process of elimination. We know *for sure* that B, C, D, and E won't work. We know *for sure* that A passes all the rules, and therefore, we know *for sure* that A is our answer. This is the proper approach to the logic games.

The Canary in the Coal Mine

This type of question, which asks you to identify a complete list of the variables in their proper spots, is an opportunity for you to make sure you understand the rules correctly. If you can't use a process of elimination to narrow it down to one and only one answer choice, then you have probably missed something about the game. When this happens, take a deep breath and start over. If you can't answer this question, you're only going to be wasting your time by proceeding to the other questions in this game.

2

QUESTION 2:

The two workers who drive the cars CANNOT be

A) Faith and Gus ⟵·· World 4 & 2.
B) Faith and Kenneth ⟵·· World 3.
C) Faith and Lisa ⟵·· World 2.
D) Gus and Kenneth ⟵·· World 1.
E) Kenneth and Lisa ⟶ What about **H**?

This question is made easy by our four worlds. We're asked to find a pair who can't ever drive simultaneously. That means any pair who *can* drive simultaneously in any of my worlds can't be the correct answer.

REFERENCE DIAGRAMS

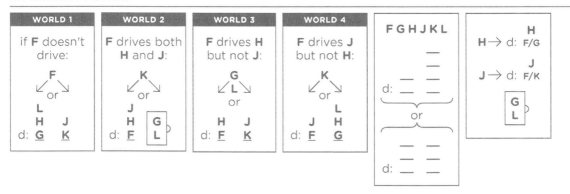

A) F and G are the two drivers in World 4, and can also be the two drivers in World 2, so this isn't the answer.
B) F and K are the two drivers in World 3, so it's not this one.
C) F and L can be the two drivers in World 2. This is out.
D) G and K are the two drivers in World 1, so this can't be it.
E) K and L can't be the two drivers in any world. If K and L were the drivers, who would drive for H? That means E is our answer.

QUESTION 3:

3

If Lisa drives one of the cars, then which one of the following could be true?

A) Faith travels in the same car as Kenneth.
B) Faith travels in the same car as Lisa.
C) Gus travels in the same car as Hannah.
D) Gus travels in the same car as Juan.
E) Hannah travels in the same car as Lisa.

Lisa can only drive in World 2. So I made a new diagram, next to Question 3, that's a version of World 2 with L driving her car. Note that K can still drive in either car.

A) This looks like the answer, since K can go in either car.
B) F and L are the two drivers in opposite cars.
C) G and H are in opposite cars.
D) G and J are in opposite cars.
E) H and L are in opposite cars, leaving A as our answer.

QUESTION 4:

4

If Faith travels with two other workers in car 1, and if Faith is not the driver, then the person in car 1 other than Faith and the driver must be

A) Gus
B) Hannah
C) Juan
D) Kenneth
E) Lisa

The only way for F to *not* drive is in World 1, where G drives H and L, and K drives J in the other car. The only way for F to ride "with two other workers" would be for F to pile in with K and J. So the person in that car "other than F and the driver" is J. Our answer is C.

QUESTION 5:

Which one of the following CANNOT be true?

A) Gus is the only person other than the driver in one of the cars.
B) Hannah is the only person other than the driver in one of the cars.
C) Juan is the only person other than the driver in one of the cars.
D) Kenneth is the only person other than the driver in one of the cars.
E) Lisa is the only person other than the driver in one of the cars.

This is a must-be-false question. You can't answer or diagram in advance, so your plan of attack is to just look through the answer choices and find one that's not possible based on your rules and inferences. Any answer that could work in any conceivable scenario can't be the correct answer.

A) This could happen in World 2.
B) This could happen in World 3.
C) This could happen in World 1, 3, or 4.
D) This can't happen in World 1 because K drives. This can't happen in World 2 because there are already 2 people in each car, before K sits down. (We're getting warmer...) This can't happen in World 3 because K drives. (The moment of truth...) This can't happen in World 4 because there are at least 2 people in each car before K sits down. Since this can't happen in any world, it's got to be the answer.
E) This could happen in World 2. Our answer is D.

How Sure Are You?

Late in the game (like here at Question 5), if you're 100% confident that D really must be false, you might choose D without even reading E. I don't advocate this early in the game because you might be misunderstanding something about the way the game works, and that's going to hurt you on later questions. Remember, you're really only saving about five seconds by not reading E. So use this technique with caution. And this is only ever acceptable on the Logic Games—you must read all five answer choices in the other sections.

Game Two

An archaeologist has six ancient artifacts—a figurine, a headdress, a jar, a necklace, a plaque, and a tureen—no two of which are the same age. She will order them from first (oldest) to sixth (most recent). The following has already been determined:

The figurine is older than both the jar and the headdress.
The necklace and the jar are both older than the tureen.
Either the plaque is older than both the headdress and the necklace, or both the headdress and the necklace are older than the plaque.

Game Two Explanation (Questions 6–11)

Ahh, right at home with a very familiar type of game. All we're asked to do is put things in order. There are six variables and six spots. Everything has to go once and only once. (Nothing can go twice, and nothing can be left out.)

First, I created a diagram below with Rules 1 and 2 combined—since they share the common variable of J—by making a pictorial representation of the first rule, then adding Rule 2 to that diagram. I left Rule 3 separate since it has an *or* in it. The *or* means we don't have an exact relationship between these variables. We're going to have to leave this rule loose for now, then apply it to each of the questions.

The last thing I do before going to the questions is ask myself "Who can go first?" and "Who can go last?" Looks like F, N, and P can go first (everyone else must be preceded by at least one other variable) and T, H, and P can go last (everyone else must be followed by at least one other variable). We haven't done a lot here, but it feels like it's time to proceed to the questions.

REFERENCE DIAGRAMS

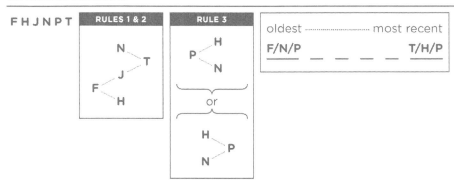

QUESTION 6:

Which one of the following could be the artifacts in the order of their age, from first to sixth?

A) figurine, headdress, jar, necklace, plaque, tureen
B) figurine, jar, plaque, headdress, tureen, necklace
C) figurine, necklace, plaque, headdress, jar, tureen
D) necklace, jar, figurine, headdress, plaque, tureen
E) plaque, tureen, figurine, necklace, jar, headdress

We'll solve this by process of elimination. Just take the first rule and eliminate as many answer choices as possible, then use the second rule to eliminate as many of the remaining answer choices as possible, and so on, until we're left with just one answer.

Rule 1: Answer D is eliminated because J is before F. All the other answers are intact.
Rule 2: Answer B is eliminated because T is before N. Answer E is also eliminated because T is before both N and J. We're down to A and C.
Rule 3: Answer C is eliminated because P is between H and N. (It's supposed to be before both, or after both, but not in between them.) Answer A doesn't violate any rules, and all the other answers have been eliminated, so we know for sure that A is our answer.

7

QUESTION 7:

Exactly how many of the artifacts are there any one of which could be first?

A) one
B) two
C) three
D) four
E) five

Before we went to the questions, we determined that F, N, and P could each go first. So three is our answer. It's C. Easy, huh? This is why we take some time making a diagram *before* going on to the questions.

QUESTION 8:

Which one of the following artifacts CANNOT be fourth?

A) figurine
B) headdress
C) jar
D) necklace
E) plaque

You can answer this question in advance by looking at our combined Rules 1 and 2. Because F has to go before J, H, and T, it can't possibly go fourth. Our answer is A. Again, this situation reminds us why diagramming so important.

SECTION **THREE**

QUESTION 9:

If the figurine is third, which one of the following must be second?

A) headdress
B) jar
C) necklace
D) plaque
E) tureen

I made a new diagram next to Question 9 incorporating the new piece of information that F must go third here. (Remember the solitaire analogy—since we have a new piece of information, everything's different now.) If F is third, then H, J, and T must take the 4-6 spots (because of Rules 1 and 2). That leaves P and N for the first two spots. Looking at Rule 3, I know that P can't go in between H and N. Since P has to go before H here (if H is in the last three spots) then P also has to go before N. So P takes the first spot, and N is in the second spot. Our answer, therefore, is C.

QUESTION 10:

If the plaque is first, then exactly how many artifacts are there any one of which could be second?

A) one
B) two
C) three
D) four
E) five

I made a new diagram next to question 10 with P in the first spot. If P is first, then Rule 3 has been satisfied because P is going to be before both H and N, no matter where they go. The question asks who can go second, so we need to look toward Rules 1 and 2 to answer it. Use the process of elimination. H can't go because F hasn't gone yet. Same for J and T. There's no reason why N and F can't go second, so our answer is two. That means B is correct.

QUESTION 11:

Which one of the following, if substituted for the information that the necklace and the jar are both older than the tureen, would have the same effect in determining the order of the artifacts?

A) The tureen is older than the headdress but not as old as the figurine.
B) The figurine and the necklace are both older than the tureen.
C) The necklace is older than the tureen if and only if the jar is.
D) All of the artifacts except the headdress and the plaque must be older than the tureen.
E) The plaque is older than the necklace if and only if the plaque is older than the tureen.

Occasionally, the last question in a given game will change the rules somehow. Here, the question asks you to identify a new rule that, if substituted for an existing rule, would lead to the exact same outcome. My first advice for a question like this is very simple: Skip it entirely! Seriously. These questions tend to be both more difficult and more

Be Wary of Perfection

Most people aren't trying for a perfect games score. The best strategy is to maximize your expected score for the section. (This isn't the same thing.) Don't let the perfect be the enemy of the good! Getting your best score is all that matters, so skip this question if it's best for you to skip it. Only you can possibly know for sure, but I'd say 90% of all test-takers should be skipping a final question that changes the rules.

time consuming than the average question. Furthermore, even if you answer this question correctly you haven't increased your knowledge of the game in a way that will benefit you on future questions, because—wait for it—this is the last question! Most students should just bubble something in and move on. If you have time at the end of the section, you can always come back to it.

Since you may be one of the brave souls trying for a perfect score on the games, let's attempt to answer this beast. (Also, can you take care of my taxes for me?) What you're looking for is a new rule that, when substituted for the old rules, leads to the exact same effects. This means the new rule can have no more *and* no less effect than the old rules. So we're going to use the process of elimination to find the correct answer.

I have two criteria: First, the new rule can do no more than the old rules. So every answer choice, in order to remain in contention, *must be true* according to the old rules. Any answer choice that does not have to be true according to the old rules has gone too far, and can be eliminated.

Second, the new rule can do no less than the old rules. So every answer choice, in order to remain in contention, can allow no more flexibility than the old rules. Any answer choice that allows for outcomes that were impossible under the old rules can be chopped.

A) This is eliminated by Criterion 1 because, according to the old rules, T does not have to be older than H. (There is no relationship between T and H according to the old rules.)
B) This must be true according to the old rules, so it survives Criterion 1. However, it leaves open the possibility that T could be before J, which was impossible under the old rules. I can eliminate it using Criterion 2.
C) This must be true according to the old rules, so it survives Criterion 1. But it leaves open the possibility that both N and J can be after T, which is impossible according to the old rules, so it's eliminated using Criterion 2.
D) This must be true according to the old rules, so it passes Criteria 1. And it doesn't allow for any possibilities that weren't available under the old rules, so it makes it through Criterion 2. It's probably the correct answer.
E) This doesn't have to be true according to the old rules, so it fails Criterion 1. Our answer is D.

If you understand all this, well, that's fantastic. But question 11 is a very hard question type. Honestly, most people should probably just guess and invest the saved time in the next game.

REFERENCE DIAGRAMS

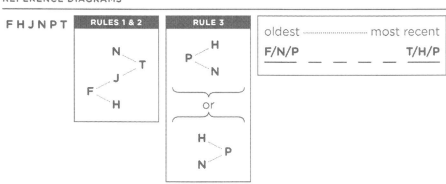

Game Three

The coach of a women's track team must determine which four of five runners—Quinn, Ramirez, Smith, Terrell, and Uzoma—will run in the four races of an upcoming track meet. Each of the four runners chosen will run in exactly one of the four races—the first, second, third, or fourth. The coach's selection is bound by the following constraints:

If Quinn runs in the track meet, then Terrell runs in the race immediately after the race in which Quinn runs.

Smith does not run in either the second race or the fourth race.

If Uzoma does not run in the track meet, then Ramirez runs in the second race.

If Ramirez runs in the second race, then Uzoma does not run in the track meet.

Game Three Explanation (Questions 12–17)

This game is much easier than it looks. It seems as if we have to do two operations: 1) select a team, and 2) rank that team. But really, all we're doing is putting five people into five spots. The spots are 1, 2, 3, 4, and OUT. No big deal.

Rule 1 indicates that Q is going to be difficult to seat, which is ultimately good for us. (Games are harder when there is more flexibility, easier when there is less flexibility.) If Q is in one of the ranked spots, then T must go immediately after it. The first inference we can make from this is that Q can't go in spot #4, because there is no spot #5.

Rule 2 is very straightforward. S can't go second or fourth. I've incorporated this into the diagram.

Rules 3 and 4 can be combined into an "if and only if" rule where if U is out, then R is in spot #2—and vice versa. So if U is not out, then R is not in spot #2. This incorporates all the pieces of Rules 3 and 4.

Before going to the questions, I decided to make four worlds based on Q (see below). You could also complete this game efficiently by making worlds based on R or S. It might be worth your while to try penciling these out just to see what would happen, but for this example, we're rolling with Q.

World 1: If Q goes first, then I know that T goes second. If T is second, then R is not second, which means that U can't be out. So either S or R is out. It's U or R in the fourth spot, because S can never go fourth.

World 2: Very similar to World 1. If Q goes second, then T goes third. If Q is second, then R isn't second, which means that U can't be out. So it's either S or R in the out spot. It's U or R in the fourth spot, because S can never go fourth.

World 3: If Q goes third, then T goes fourth. Only R or U can go second, because S can never go second. Either S, R, or U can go fourth.

World 4: Q is out. If Q is out, then U is not out. If U is not out, then R cannot be second. S can never be second, so only U or T is left for the second spot.

This isn't the only diagram we could have made, but the point is that we've

REFERENCE DIAGRAMS

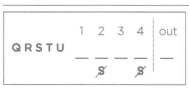

armed ourselves with at least *some* weapons before attacking the questions. You may have done something completely different and done quite well on the game. But it's doubtful that you did the game efficiently if you went directly to the questions. Usually, the game will ambush you if you take this approach.

QUESTION 12:

12

Which one of the following could be the order in which the runners run, from first to fourth?

A) Uzoma, Ramirez, Quinn, Terrell
B) Terrell, Smith, Ramirez, Uzoma
C) Smith, Ramirez, Terrell, Quinn
D) Ramirez, Uzoma, Smith, Terrell
E) Quinn, Terrell, Smith, Ramirez

Process of elimination. Take each rule, in order, and eliminate as many answer choices as you can with it. There will only be one answer choice standing at the end of this process.

Rule 1: C is eliminated because Q is ranked but T does not immediately follow it.
Rule 2: B is eliminated because S cannot run second.
Rule 3: E is eliminated because U is out but R is not second.
Rule 4: A is eliminated because R is second but U is not out.

Answer choice D meets all of the criteria in the rules while A, B, C, and E violate them. D is therefore our answer.

QUESTION 13:

13

Which one of the following runners must the coach select to run in the track meet?

A) Quinn
B) Ramirez
C) Smith
D) Terrell
E) Uzoma

Here, we only need to scan down the "out" spot in our four worlds to see that T can never be out in any world. If T can't be out in any world, then T must be included in every world—so the answer is D.

Minding Your Ts and Qs

An alternative, more intuitive approach here would have been to recognize that T is *necessary* for Q, and there is only one out spot. If T were out, then Q would have to be in, but Q can't be in without T. Therefore T must always be in. It's a useful inference, and this approach would have worked whether or not you diagrammed the worlds.

14

QUESTION 14:

The question of which runners will be chosen to run in the track meet and in what races they will run can be completely resolved if which one of the following is true?

A) Ramirez runs in the first race.
B) Ramirez runs in the second race.
C) Ramirez runs in the third race.
D) Ramirez runs in the fourth race.
E) Ramirez does not run in the track meet.

This question asks for a trigger that will completely determine the outcome of the game. Let's look for something that forces at least one other thing to happen, and see if a chain of events causes all the pieces to fall into place.

Every answer asks about R, so before we start testing answer choices, spend some time thinking about what you know about R. We know that if R is second, then U has to be out. That's Rule 4. If U is out, then Q has to be in. If Q is in, then QT will have to be in. If R is second, then QT will have to be third and fourth, which will leave only S for the first spot. So R in the second spot is the answer. That means B must be our guy.

15

QUESTION 15:

Which one of the following CANNOT be true?

A) Ramirez runs in the race immediately before the race in which Smith runs.
B) Smith runs in the race immediately before the race in which Quinn runs.
C) Smith runs in the race immediately before the race in which Terrell runs.
D) Terrell runs in the race immediately before the race in which Ramirez runs.
E) Uzoma runs in the race immediately before the race in which Terrell runs.

We can't answer this one in advance, because we're not given any new information, or even asked about a particular person or particular spot. We're going to look for an answer choice that causes problems. If we can prove an answer choice is impossible, then that's the answer.

A) This can't happen in any of my worlds, so it's the answer. In World 1, S can only be ranked if it is third, with T before it in the second spot. In Worlds 2 and 3, S can only be ranked if it is first (with nobody in front of it). In World 4, S can go first or third. If it's third, only U or T can immediately precede it. That means A has to be our answer.
B) This could happen in World 2.
C) This could happen in World 4.
D) This could happen in Worlds 1 and 4.
E) This could happen in World 4. So, yep—it's A.

16

QUESTION 16:

If Uzoma runs in the first race, then which one of the following must be true?

A) Quinn does not run in the track meet.
B) Smith does not run in the track meet.
C) Quinn runs in the second race.
D) Terrell runs in the second race.
E) Ramirez runs in the fourth race.

Based on the worlds we've made, this is the hardest question in the game. If you did different worlds, you might have found it easier. But we're stuck with what we've got at this point—onward!

My immediate inference was that if U is first then it's not out, which means R cannot be second. Still, it initially appears as if U could be in the first spot in Worlds 2, 3, and 4—which is *not* what I was hoping for. (It would be much easier to answer the question if U could only go first in one of my worlds.) So I penciled these worlds out. In World 2, if U is first and QT are third and fourth, then S must be out (because the first and third spots are occupied), which leaves only R for the fourth spot. This world works.

In World 3, (with QT in the third and fourth spots) if you look closely you'll realize that nobody was going to be able to go second. S can never go there, and R can't go there unless U is out. So this world doesn't work. Cross it out.

In World 4, if Q is out then S has to be in. The only place that will work for S is the third spot. R can't go second, so it must go fourth, which leaves T for the second spot. Now we can evaluate the answer choices. Since we're looking for something that *must be true*, we have to find something that must be true in *both* of my remaining worlds. (World 2 and World 4.)

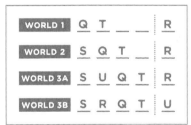

A) Q runs in World 2, so this is out.
B) S runs in World 4, so this is out.
C) Q doesn't run at all in World 4, so this is out.
D) T runs third in World 2, so this is out.
E) R runs fourth in both Worlds 2 and 4, so this is the correct answer.

QUESTION 17:

If both Quinn and Smith run in the track meet, then how many of the runners are there any one of whom could be the one who runs in the first race?

A) one
B) two
C) three
D) four
E) five

Q and S can both run in Worlds 1, 2, and 3. So let's make versions of those three worlds where both Q and S run. In World 1, Q goes first. In World 2, if R is out then S has to run. The third spot is already taken by Q, so S has to go first. In World 3, no matter whether R or U is out, S will have to go in the first spot. So only Q and S can go first if both Q and S run. Our answer is B.

REFERENCE DIAGRAMS

Game Four

From the 1st through the 7th of next month, seven nurses—Farnham, Griseldi, Heany, Juarez, Khan, Lightfoot, and Moreau—will each conduct one information session at a community center. Each nurse's session will fall on a different day. The nurses' schedule is governed by the following constraints:
At least two of the other nurses' sessions must fall in between Heany's session and Moreau's session.
Griseldi's session must be on the day before Khan's.
Juarez's session must be on a later day than Moreau's.
Farnham's session must be on an earlier day than Khan's but on a later day than Lightfoot's.
Lightfoot cannot conduct the session on the 2nd.

Game Four Explanation (Questions 18–23)

I love this game.

I love it because it rewards people who have practiced a lot for the LSAT and have learned to read the tea leaves. This game is all or nothing—it's very difficult for people who haven't had enough practice on the games, and it's very easy for people who have. I'll show you what I mean in a second.

It's a basic ordering game. We have seven variables, each of which must go once and only once, in order, with no ties. Rules 2 and 4 can be combined into L... F... GK. It's tempting to try to link Rules 1 and 3, but since Rule 1 can be either H _ _ ... M or M _ _ ... H, we can't really be sure where J will go, so it's best to leave them apart.

The last rule is my favorite. It seems like the tiniest little thing: L can't go second. But it turns out to be incredibly important. If L can't go second, then where *can* L go? It can't go in the last three spots because it has to precede F, G, and K. So it seems like it could go only first, third, or fourth.

But when we pencil out these three worlds, you'll notice that the last one won't work! If L goes fourth, then FGK have to take up the last three spots, which leaves no room for M _ _ ...H or H _ _ ... M. So actually, L can only go in two places, first or third.

And we're not even done yet. If L goes third, then F, G, and K have to take up three of the last four spots. The remaining spot in the last four must be either M or H, in order to space M and H out from each other. And since M must precede J, it has to be H in the last four spots with F, G, and K.

M and J, then, must take the first two spots and in that exact order. If M is first, then H can go in any spot 4 through 7, with F ... GK taking up the other three spots. Thus the world in which L is third is almost entirely complete.

The world in which L is first has a lot of flexibility, but you don't have to worry much about that. The game has already been almost completely conquered by the realization that either L goes first or it's MJL (H, F... GK). The last rule was the clue, and if you practice enough for the games, you'll start to see the clues when they are offered.

REFERENCE DIAGRAMS

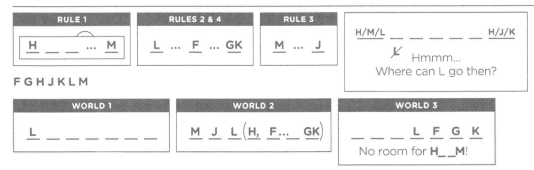

QUESTION 18:

Which one of the following could be the order of the nurses' sessions, from first to last?

A) Farnham, Griseldi, Khan, Moreau, Juarez, Lightfoot, Heany
B) Heany, Lightfoot, Farnham, Moreau, Juarez, Griseldi, Khan
C) Juarez, Heany, Lightfoot, Farnham, Moreau, Griseldi, Khan
D) Lightfoot, Moreau, Farnham, Juarez, Griseldi, Khan, Heany
E) Moreau, Lightfoot, Heany, Juarez, Farnham, Griseldi, Khan

Let's ignore our totally awesome diagram for this question only. Once again we're going to use the rules, in order, to eliminate answer choices.

Rule 1: E is eliminated because H and M are too close together.
Rule 2: This doesn't eliminate any of the remaining answer choices.
Rule 3: C is eliminated because J is before M.
Rule 4: A is eliminated because F is before L.
Rule 5: B is eliminated because L is second.

Because A, B, C, and E have been eliminated, and because D has met all of the requirements, D is our answer. Good start, and we still have the secret weapon in our back pocket.

QUESTION 19:

Juarez's session CANNOT be on which one of the following days?

A) the 2nd
B) the 3rd
C) the 5th
D) the 6th
E) the 7th

This question is on the tougher side. We have to test answer choices until we find one that breaks.

A) We know J can go second because of World 2, so there's no need to test this answer.
B) If J goes in 3, then L has to go first because L can only go first or third. M would then go second, and F would go fourth (because H would be too close to M, and everyone else has to go after F), but this ended up working out—so it's not the answer.
C) If J is fifth, then L goes first because if L is third it forces J to be second. So we have L _ _ _ J _ _. We can't put GK in the last two spots, because if we do we won't have room to spread M and H out far enough. And we can't put FGK in 2-4 for the same reason. Therefore J can't go fifth. This is probably our answer.
D) We don't need to bother testing this because we already know J can't go fifth.
E) Same as D. We're left with C as the correct answer.

20

QUESTION 20:

If Juarez's session is on the 3rd, then which one of the following could be true?

A) Moreau's session is on the 1st.
B) Khan's session is on the 5th.
C) Heany's session is on the 6th.
D) Griseldi's session is on the 5th.
E) Farnham's session is on the 2nd.

J has to be second in World 2, so in order for J to be third we have to be in World 1. So it's L _ J _ _ _ _. If that's true, then M has to go second, so it's LMJ _ _ _ _. The only player that could go fourth at that point is F. So it's LMJF(H, GK).

A) Nope, M goes second.
B) Nope, K can go either sixth or seventh.
C) Nope, H can go either fifth or seventh.
D) Yep, G can go fifth if K goes sixth and H goes seventh. This is probably our answer.
E) Nope, F goes fourth. Our answer is D.

21

QUESTION 21:

If Khan's session is on an earlier day than Moreau's, which one of the following could conduct the session on the 3rd?

A) Griseldi
B) Heany
C) Juarez
D) Lightfoot
E) Moreau

In order for K to be earlier than M, we have to be in World 1. (K is after M in World 2.) So we have L in the first spot, and F … GK … M… J. The only floater is H, which has to be at least two spaces away from M. It can't be after J because there's nobody else to fill an additional spot behind M, so it will have to be before GK or before F and GK. So my finished diagram is L (H,F) GKMJ. The question asks who could go third. Either H or F *could* go third, but only one of them is listed, H. So our answer is B.

REFERENCE DIAGRAMS

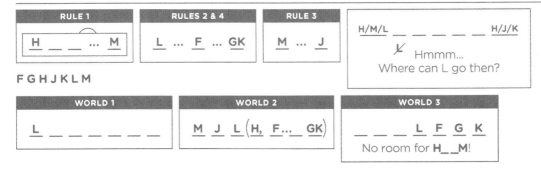

QUESTION 22:

If Griseldi's session is on the 5th, then which one of the following must be true?

A) Farnham's session is on the 3rd.
B) Heany's session is on the 7th.
C) Juarez's session is on the 4th.
D) Lightfoot's session is on the 1st.
E) Moreau's session is on the 2nd.

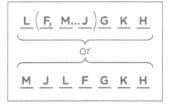

G can be fifth in either World 1 or 2, so let's pencil out both scenarios. (See right.) The question asks for something that must be true, so we're looking for an answer choice that has to be true in both scenarios.

A) F doesn't have to be third in either scenario, so this is a bad answer.
B) H has to be seventh in both scenarios, so this is probably going to end up as our answer.
C) J could be fourth in the first scenario, but doesn't have to be fourth in either scenario. No way.
D) L is first in the first scenario, but is third in the other scenario. This is out.
E) M doesn't have to be second in either world, so this is out. Our answer is B.

QUESTION 23:

Lightfoot's session could be on which one of the following days?

A) the 3rd
B) the 4th
C) the 5th
D) the 6th
E) the 7th

Easiest question in the game. L can only go first or third. Only one of these is listed, so our answer is A. Thank you, secret weapon.

SECTION
FOUR

Logical Reasoning

(Or: Another 35 Minutes of Outrage)

There's no difference between the first and second sections of Logical Reasoning. Yes, one LR section will probably seem more difficult than the other one to any given test taker, but two test takers are likely to disagree on which one was the hard one. It's pointless to worry about it, so just do your best for 35 minutes.

Remember: 1) Get mad at the speakers—they're usually trying to pull a fast one on you. 2) Answer the questions *before* looking at the answer choices whenever possible.

QUESTION 1:

Among Trinidadian guppies, males with large spots are more attractive to females than are males with small spots, who consequently are presented with less frequent mating opportunities. Yet guppies with small spots are more likely to avoid detection by predators, so in waters where predators are abundant only guppies with small spots live to maturity.

The situation described above most closely conforms to which one of the following generalizations?

A) A trait that helps attract mates is sometimes more dangerous to one sex than to another.
B) Those organisms that are most attractive to the opposite sex have the greatest number of offspring.
C) Those organisms that survive the longest have the greatest number of offspring.
D) Whether a trait is harmful to the organisms of a species can depend on which sex possesses it.
E) A trait that is helpful to procreation can also hinder it in certain environments.

The scenario described seems to suck for both groups of male guppies. The big-spotted ones get more mating opportunities, but always get eaten by predators before maturity if there are a lot of predators around. The small-spotted ones are better at avoiding the predators, but are less attractive to the ladies. There's no logic here, just a couple of facts. So we really can't criticize or argue with anything.

The question reads: "The situation described above most closely conforms to which one of the following generalizations?" This is an "identify the principle" question. We need to look for an answer choice that matches the facts as we've described them above. The correct answer must be supported by the facts. It can't be something that is probably true, or seems to be true, but something that has evidentiary support in the passage we were given.

A) This seems confused, because there's nothing in the facts about whether having spots is more or less dangerous for females. The facts are only about males, so we want something better.
B) There's nothing about who leaves more offspring. It might seem, at first, as if the big-spotted guppies would leave more offspring because they are more at-tractive and get more frequent mating opportunities. But they also tend to get eaten by predators! The smaller-spotted guppies seem to live a long time, and they do get some mating opportunities, so maybe they actually end up leaving more offspring in the long run. But we don't know for sure, so this can't be the answer.
C) Same explanation as B. There's nothing in the facts we were given about who leaves the most offspring.
D) Same explanation as A. There's nothing in the facts we were given about males vs. females.
E) This, we know for sure. Big spots are helpful for procreation but can be a hin-drance if there are a lot of predators around. Our answer is E.

QUESTION 2:

Programmer: We computer programmers at Mytheco are demanding raises to make our average salary comparable with that of the technical writers here who receive, on average, 20 percent more in salary and benefits than we do. This pay difference is unfair and intolerable.

Mytheco executive: But many of the technical writers have worked for Mytheco longer than have many of the programmers. Since salary and benefits at Mytheco are directly tied to seniority, the 20 percent pay difference you mention is perfectly acceptable.

Evaluating the adequacy of the Mytheco executive's response requires a clarification of which one of the following?

A) whether any of the technical writers at Mytheco once worked as programmers at the company
B) how the average seniority of programmers compares with the average seniority of technical writers
C) whether the sorts of benefits an employee of Mytheco receives are tied to the salary of that employee
D) whether the Mytheco executive was at one time a technical writer employed by Mytheco
E) how the Mytheco executive's salary compares with that of the programmers

The programmer is mad because technical writers at Mytheco make, on average, 20 percent more than its programmers. The programmers, he says, are "demanding raises." The executive says "many" of the technical writers have worked for Mytheco longer than "many" of the programmers, so the pay difference is acceptable.

If I were the programmer, I might counter that most of the programmers at Mytheco have worked at the company longer than most of the technical writers! This would be entirely consistent with the executive's shady facts. The executive didn't say that *all* the technical writers have worked there longer than *all* the programmers, or even that *most* of the writers have worked there longer than *most* of the programmers. Really, all the exec has proven is that there are at least a few veteran writers and at least a few veteran programmers. But the average tenure of the programmers could still be much greater than that of the writers! Always be skeptical on the LSAT, especially when "executives" are speaking.

The question asks "Evaluating the adequacy of the Mytheco executive's response requires a clarification of which one of the following?" In other words, what facts would you need in order to claim that the executive is full of shit? I think we can answer this one in advance. We're looking for something like "the average tenure of the programmers and the tech writers." That's what I would want to know if I were in the programmer's shoes.

A) This is entirely irrelevant. No matter what the answer to this question is, it doesn't help us argue with the executive.
B) This exactly matches our advance answer, so it's a good bet. If the programmers have average seniority greater than that of the tech writers, then the executive's shady argument is totally destroyed.
C) Not what we're looking for, and B is already the perfect answer, so just skim the remaining answers at this point to make sure there's not something almost identical to B that we have to consider.
D) Not relevant.
E) Not relevant either. Good. Our answer is B.

QUESTION 3:

Cable TV stations have advantages that enable them to attract many more advertisers than broadcast networks attract. For example, cable stations are able to target particular audiences with 24-hour news, sports, or movies, whereas broadcast networks must offer a variety of programming. Cable can also offer lower advertising rates than any broadcast network can, because it is subsidized by viewers through subscriber fees. Additionally, many cable stations have expanded worldwide with multinational programming.

The statements above, if true, provide support for each of the following EXCEPT:

A) Some broadcast networks can be viewed in several countries.
B) Broadcast networks do not rely on subscriber fees from viewers.
C) Low costs are often an important factor for advertisers in selecting a station or network on which to run a TV ad.
D) Some advertisers prefer to have the opportunity to address a worldwide audience.
E) The audiences that some advertisers prefer to target watch 24-hour news stations.

The facts here are all about the advantages that cable TV stations have over broadcast networks. There's no mention of the disadvantages, but that doesn't mean there aren't any! Our advance answer at this point, before we get to the question, is something along the lines of, "Okay, that sounds great and all, but what about the disadvantages?"

The question says "The statements above, if true, provide support for each of the following EXCEPT:" In other words, four of the answer choices have been supported by the facts that were presented, and one of the answer choices (the correct answer) is something either out of the blue or contrary to the facts.

A) There is no evidence that any broadcast networks can be viewed in multiple countries (unlike some cable networks) so this is probably the answer. Let's go through the rest of the answer choices and make sure each one is supported by the facts. If they are (and hopefully they will be) then our answer is A.
B) This is suggested by the third sentence.
C) This is suggested by the first and third sentences combined.
D) This is suggested by the last sentence.
E) This is suggested by the second sentence. Our answer is A.

Note: This was an uncomfortable question for me, since I was hoping that the four incorrect answers would be *proven* by the evidence. But because A was not even suggested by the evidence (actually, it's somewhat contrary to the tone of the evidence that was given), the fact that B-E were each *suggested* by the evidence is going to have to be good enough. This horse is long dead, but I'm gonna kick it again: This is why you have to read all of the answer choices in the Logical Reasoning sections.

QUESTION 4:

In polluted industrial English cities during the Industrial Revolution, two plant diseases—black spot, which infects roses, and tar spot, which infects sycamore trees—disappeared. It is likely that air pollution eradicated these diseases.

Which one of the following, if true, most strengthens the reasoning above?

A) Scientists theorize that some plants can develop a resistance to air pollution.
B) Certain measures help prevent infection by black spot and tar spot, but once infection occurs, it is very difficult to eliminate.
C) For many plant species, scientists have not determined the effects of air pollution.
D) Black spot and tar spot returned when the air in the cities became less polluted.
E) Black spot and tar spot were the only plant diseases that disappeared in any English cities during the Industrial Revolution.

This is a correlation-equals-causation argument. English cities were polluted during the Industrial Revolution, and two plant diseases disappeared during that time. That's correlation: two things happening in tandem. But the conclusion says the pollution *caused* the plant diseases to disappear. Where's the evidence for that assertion? There is none. Many other things could have caused the plant diseases to disappear. Here's a few of them: Did plant doctors invent new plant disease cures during this time? Did a species of ladybug that eats plant fungus migrate from Spain during this time? Did the climate cool by 5 degrees, or warm by 5 degrees, thus eradicating the diseases? If any of these alternate causes are valid, then the argument is completely destroyed.

The question asks "Which one of the following, if true, most strengthens the reasoning above?" So instead of weakening, which we were just doing, we have to strengthen. What the argument desperately needs is *some* reason to believe that plant diseases don't like pollution. So "air pollution kills all plant diseases" is the ideal advance answer.

A) Nothing here about the relationship between plant diseases and pollution, so I don't see how this can strengthen the argument.
B) Nothing here about pollution, so it's out.
C) The fact that scientists "have not determined the effects" is worthless as both a strengthener and a weakener. The scientists can get back to us when they have some results. This is out.
D) This indicates that the diseases didn't like the pollution, so it's the best answer so far.
E) This doesn't do anything to strengthen the tie between the pollution and the diseases. So it's out. Our answer is D.

QUESTION 5:

Many scholars are puzzled about who created the seventeenth-century abridgment of Shakespeare's Hamlet contained in the First Quarto. Two facts about the work shed light on this question. First, the person who undertook the abridgment clearly did not possess a copy of Hamlet. Second, the abridgment contains a very accurate rendering of the speeches of one of the characters, but a slipshod handling of all the other parts.

Which one of the following statements is most supported by the information above?

A) The abridgment was prepared by Shakespeare.
B) The abridgment was created to make Hamlet easier to produce on stage.
C) The abridgment was produced by an actor who had played a role in Hamlet.
D) The abridgement was prepared by a spectator of a performance of Hamlet.
E) The abridgment was produced by an actor who was trying to improve the play.

I, frankly, do not give a damn about *Hamlet*, much less any abridgment of *Hamlet* contained in the "First Quarto" (whatever the hell that is). Maybe you do. In which case, congrats, this question should be quite pleasant for you. But the rest of us are just going to have to do our best to follow the logic. The author presents two facts about the abridgement: First, whoever did the abridgment did not have a copy of *Hamlet*. Second, the abridgment is very accurate with regard to one character but shoddy with regard to the other parts. Fair enough.

The question says "Which one of the following statements is most supported by the information above?" So we have to find an answer choice that, ideally, *must be true* according to the author's facts. If we can't find something that must be true according to the author's facts, then we're going to find something that is at least *strongly suggested* by the author's facts. Wrong answers will be speculation with no support from the facts, or will be contrary to the facts.

A) I find it unlikely that Shakespeare himself didn't have a copy of Hamlet, so this seems like a terrible answer.
B) The facts give us no idea what the purpose of the abridgment was, so this is out.
C) This seems possible, since it gets the speeches of one character right but botches the rest of the play. This is the best answer so far. Hopefully D and E both suck so we can choose C and get out of here.
D) A spectator who had the hots for one particular actor in the play, or a spectator who was one of the actors' moms, might remember very well the lines of one character and screw up on everyone else's. You can make a case for D, but it requires a bigger leap and more assumptions. C is much more straightforward, and is a more clear, solid answer, so we can eliminate D.
E) Why would an actor who was trying to improve the play leave all the lines of one actor the same but change everyone else's? C is the best answer.

QUESTION 6:

Musicologist: Many critics complain of the disproportion between text and music in Handel's *da capo* arias. These texts are generally quite short and often repeated well beyond what is needed for literal understanding. Yet such criticism is refuted by noting that repetition serves a vital function: it frees the audience to focus on the music itself, which can speak to audiences whatever their language.

Which one of the following sentences best expresses the main point of the musicologist's reasoning?

A) Handel's *da capo* arias contain a disproportionate amount of music.
B) Handel's *da capo* arias are superior to most in their accessibility to diverse audiences.
C) At least one frequent criticism of Handel's *da capo* arias is undeserved.
D) At least some of Handel's *da capo* arias contain unnecessary repetitions.
E) Most criticism of Handel's *da capo* arias is unwarranted.

I don't understand a damn thing about what the musicologist is trying to say about the criticism of Handel's arias. What I do know for sure is that the musicologist is trying to say the critics are wrong. I know this because the words "such criticism is refuted" tipped me off. Let's hope that's enough to answer the question.

A) Not what we're looking for.
B) Not what we're looking for.
C) This is the closest so far to our "the critics are wrong" advance answer. If D and E are both bad, we're going with C.
D) This seems to be what the critics are saying—not the musicologist.
E) Close, but this statement goes too far. The musicologist never said *most* criticism of Handel's arias is unwarranted, she just said one particular group of critics (those who complain about the disproportion between text and music) are wrong. C is our answer.

QUESTION 7:

Baxe Interiors, one of the largest interior design companies in existence, currently has a near monopoly in the corporate market. Several small design companies have won prestigious awards for their corporate work, while Baxe has won none. Nonetheless, the corporate managers who solicit design proposals will only contract with companies they believe are unlikely to go bankrupt, and they believe that only very large companies are unlikely to go bankrupt.

The statements above, if true, most strongly support which one of the following?

A) There are other very large design companies besides Baxe, but they produce designs that are inferior to Baxe's.
B) Baxe does not have a near monopoly in the market of any category of interior design other than corporate interiors.
C) For the most part, designs that are produced by small companies are superior to the designs produced by Baxe.
D) At least some of the corporate managers who solicit design proposals are unaware that there are designs that are much better than those produced by Baxe.
E) The existence of interior designs that are superior to those produced by Baxe does not currently threaten its near monopoly in the corporate market.

The facts that we're presented are that Baxe is very large, and enjoys a "near monopoly" in the corporate interior design market. The reason Baxe is chosen so frequently by corporate managers isn't necessarily because they are the best (smaller firms win all the awards) but because corporate managers like going with a big firm that won't go bankrupt.

The question asks me to identify something that has been proven, or is very likely to be true, based *only* on the facts as provided. Outside information is no good here. I know I keep harping on this point, but it really is that important. And I wouldn't keep harping on it if it didn't come up on so many questions. Let's go.

A) We were given no evidence about the quality of other large firms' designs. This is out.
B) We were given no evidence about whether Baxe operates in any other categories of interior design. Maybe they do, maybe they don't. This is out too.
C) We know small companies have won awards, but that isn't the same thing as being objectively superior. Awards can sometimes be totally unrelated to actual merit (see: *Titanic* winning the Oscar for Best Picture) (actually, see: just about every Oscar race ever). This comes off like a trap for the lazy; there has to be something better.
D) The managers might be fully aware that smaller firms produce better designs and still choose the inferior designs of larger firms, because they might prefer the certainty that comes from going with a huge firm unlikely to go bankrupt, which was mentioned in the premise. This is out.
E) Baxe "currently has a near monopoly" so regardless of whatever else is going on in the market (awards be damned), their near monopoly isn't being threatened. That's more like it. Our answer is E.

QUESTION 8:

The giant Chicxulub crater in Mexico provides indisputable evidence that a huge asteroid, about six miles across, struck Earth around the time many of the last dinosaur species were becoming extinct. But this catastrophe was probably not responsible for most of these extinctions. Any major asteroid strike kills many organisms in or near the region of the impact, but there is little evidence that such a strike could have a worldwide effect. Indeed, some craters even larger than the Chicxulub crater were made during times in Earth's history when there were no known extinctions.

Which one of the following, if true, would most weaken the argument?

A) The vast majority of dinosaur species are known to have gone extinct well before the time of the asteroid impact that produced the Chicxulub crater.
B) The size of a crater caused by an asteroid striking Earth generally depends on both the size of that asteroid and the force of its impact.
C) Fossils have been discovered of a number of dinosaurs that clearly died as a result of the asteroid impact that produced the Chicxulub crater.
D) There is no evidence that any other asteroid of equal size struck Earth at the same time as the asteroid that produced the Chicxulub crater.
E) During the period immediately before the asteroid that produced the Chicxulub crater struck, most of the world's dinosaurs lived in or near the region of the asteroid's impending impact.

The first thing to notice in this question is the word "indisputable." This is like someone saying "clearly" or "obviously"—these words are usually used by blowhards that are trying to ram something down our throats. I'm always skeptical on the LSAT, but "indisputable" makes me particularly angry. That's a good thing.

The argument seems to say that because many bigger asteroid strikes haven't been associated with extinctions, this particular asteroid strike isn't responsible for the extinctions that happened around the same time as the strike. This is a little like saying that because many gunshot wounds don't lead to deaths, this particular dead guy can't have been killed by a gunshot no matter what. I don't buy it.

The argument is pretty poor, because it doesn't even posit a possible alternate cause. If the asteroid strike didn't cause the extinctions, well, what did? The speaker is silent on this point. To weaken the argument all we need is some evidence that ties together the asteroid strike and the extinctions.

A) If the extinctions happened before the asteroid strike, this would strengthen the argument rather than weaken it. This is out for sure.
B) The size of the crater is completely irrelevant. No way.
C) This directly ties some of the dinosaur deaths to the asteroid strike. If nothing better comes along, this will be our answer.
D) Lack of another asteroid isn't a very good weakener here, since the author seems to say that asteroids generally can't cause extinctions. Lack of other possible alternate causes might help, but this doesn't do anything.
E) This is even better than C. The author acknowledges that asteroids can wipe out life in a local area. If it's true that most of the world's dinosaurs were living in or near the impact, then the author would have to acknowledge that the impact could have killed off most of the world's dinosaurs. Answer C doesn't quite get there because the author would say "of course there are several fossils in the local impact area, I am saying this can't have led to global extinctions." The author has no such rejoinder to answer E. Tough question, but E is our answer.

QUESTION 9:

In a sample containing 1,000 peanuts from lot A and 1,000 peanuts from lot B, 50 of the peanuts from lot A were found to be infected with *Aspergillus*. Two hundred of the peanuts from lot B were found to be infected with *Aspergillus*. Therefore, infection with *Aspergillus* is more widespread in lot B than in lot A.

The reasoning in which one of the following is most similar to the reasoning in the argument above?

A) Every one of these varied machine parts is of uniformly high quality. Therefore, the machine that we assemble from them will be of equally high quality.
B) If a plant is carelessly treated, it is likely to develop blight. If a plant develops blight, it is likely to die. Therefore, if a plant is carelessly treated, it is likely to die.
C) In the past 1,000 experiments, whenever an experimental fungicide was applied to coffee plants infected with coffee rust, the infection disappeared. The coffee rust never disappeared before the fungicide was applied. Therefore, in these experiments, application of the fungicide caused the disappearance of coffee rust.
D) Three thousand registered voters—1,500 members of the Liberal party and 1,500 members of the Conservative party—were asked which mayoral candidate they favored. Four hundred of the Liberals and 300 of the Conservatives favored Pollack. Therefore, Pollack has more support among Liberals than among Conservatives.
E) All of my livestock are registered with the regional authority. None of the livestock registered with the regional authority are free-range livestock. Therefore, none of my livestock are free-range livestock.

This argument stands to reason, because random sampling is a widely accepted scientific tool. Samples of 1,000 were taken from both lot A and lot B. The sample taken from lot B had more infections than the sample taken from lot A. Therefore, the conclusion states, Lot B as a whole must have more infections than lot A as a whole. My only concern is that it is not specified that these are *random* samples. However, unless there is some reason to believe the samples were poorly—*i.e.*, non-randomly—selected (and here we aren't given any such information) then the logic is pretty sound.

The question asks us to identify a similar pattern of reasoning. What we need to look for is a similar sampling-based argument. Because the reasoning in the given argument is sound based on what we know, the reasoning in the correct answer will also have to be sound.

A) There's no sampling here. Also, the logic is flawed: It is entirely possible to put together a shitty machine out of top-quality parts. (Some NBA "Dream Teams" come to mind.) This is out.
B) This is conditional reasoning, and there was no conditional reasoning in the argument we were presented. We're looking for sampling, and there's no sampling here. This is out.
C) This is a cause-and-effect argument, and there was no cause-and-effect in the argument we were presented. We need sampling, and there's no sampling here. This is out.
D) This has sampling in it, and the logic seems to be sound. This must be it.
E) This is conditional reasoning, and there was no conditional reasoning in the argument we were presented. No sampling here. This is out. Our answer is D.

QUESTION 10:

Economist: If the belief were to become widespread that losing one's job is not a sign of personal shortcomings but instead an effect of impersonal social forces (which is surely correct), there would be growth in the societal demand for more government control of the economy to protect individuals from these forces, just as the government now protects them from military invasion. Such extensive government control of the economy would lead to an economic disaster, however.

The economist's statements, if true, most strongly support which one of the following?

A) Increased knowledge of the causes of job loss could lead to economic disaster.
B) An individual's belief in his or her own abilities is the only reliable protection against impersonal social forces.
C) Governments should never interfere with economic forces.
D) Societal demand for government control of the economy is growing.
E) In general, people should feel no more responsible for economic disasters than for military invasions.

The logic of this passage is a little loose. If a certain belief were to become widespread, the author claims that societal demand for a certain type of government control would grow. There is no evidence presented for this assertion. Then the author claims (again without evidence) that if such government control were to happen extensively, it would lead to economic disaster. There are so many holes in this argument that it's hard to know where to begin.

The question really bails us out here by telling us to assume that the economist's statements are true. This means we no longer have to question the economist—everything he has claimed is now turned into fact. All we have to do is find an answer choice that is supported by those facts. It can be tricky to get in this mindset since we've already poked holes in his logic, but it's really as simple as that.

A) This seems to be exactly what the economist is saying. It's a leap, but we're playing by his rules now, so this is the answer unless something else jumps out at us.
B) This isn't what the economist is saying at all. Where is the prediction of disaster? No way.
C) This goes much further than the economist's claims. The economist mentioned one specific type of government control that would cause disaster; he never said that all government interference is bad.
D) The economist says this would happen *if* people changed their beliefs about what causes job loss. The economist didn't say this is happening right now.
E) The argument is not about what we should and shouldn't feel responsible for. The economist was making a prediction, and that prediction is best captured by answer A.

11

QUESTION 11:

A development company has proposed building an airport near the city of Dalton. If the majority of Dalton's residents favor the proposal, the airport will be built. However, it is unlikely that a majority of Dalton's residents would favor the proposal, for most of them believe that the airport would create noise problems. Thus, it is unlikely that the airport will be built.

The reasoning in the argument is flawed in that the argument

A) treats a sufficient condition for the airport's being built as a necessary condition

B) concludes that something must be true, because most people believe it to be true

C) concludes, on the basis that a certain event is unlikely to occur, that the event will not occur

D) fails to consider whether people living near Dalton would favor building the airport

E) overlooks the possibility that a new airport could benefit the local economy

This question lays down a classic error of conditional reasoning, and it's been tested over, and over, and over on the LSAT. It's critical that you understand this error.

The error is basically this: If you're named Tim Lincecum, then you're on the San Francisco Giants. But this player isn't named Tim Lincecum, so this player isn't a San Francisco Giant. (Wait a minute, what if this player is Buster Posey?) Another example: If you're at In-N-Out Burger, then you are going to get a damn tasty burger. But you're not at In-N-Out Burger, so no tasty burgers for you. (Wait a minute, aren't there other places that serve tasty burgers?)

On the LSAT, this is called "confusing a sufficient condition for a necessary condition." If your name is Tim Lincecum, then that's *sufficient information* for me to know you're a San Francisco Giant. But it's not *necessary* for you to be named Tim Lincecum in order to be a Giant.

Same thing with the argument in Question 11. If a majority of residents favor the proposal, then that's sufficient information for us to know that the airport will be built. The argument then acts as if a majority is necessary for the airport to be built. But what if the mayor decides it should be built anyway? There is no evidence provided that says it's impossible to build without majority approval. The argument's conclusion that the airport will not be built doesn't follow from the facts in the argument.

A) And here we are. Voter approval is sufficient, but the argument has treated it as necessary. Thanks to Tim Lincecum and In-N-Out, we knew this was the answer well before we went to the answer choices. We still need to scan the rest of the answer choices before moving on, but we can do it quickly since this one is so good. The LSAT confuses sufficient and necessary conditions all the time. When you identify that flaw in an argument, you can be fairly sure it has to be the correct answer.

B) I don't think the argument does this.

C) The conclusion says "unlikely" so the argument doesn't do this.

D) This is totally irrelevant to the argument.

E) The economy is not a factor here. As expected, our answer is A.

QUESTION 12:

After the rush-hour speed limit on the British M25 motorway was lowered from 70 miles per hour (115 kilometers per hour) to 50 miles per hour (80 kilometers per hour), rush-hour travel times decreased by approximately 15 percent.

Which one of the following, if true, most helps to explain the decrease in travel times described above?

A) After the decrease in the rush-hour speed limit, the average speed on the M25 was significantly lower during rush hours than at other times of the day.
B) Travel times during periods other than rush hours were essentially unchanged after the rush-hour speed limit was lowered.
C) Before the rush-hour speed limit was lowered, rush-hour accidents that caused lengthy delays were common, and most of these accidents were caused by high-speed driving.
D) Enforcement of speed limits on the M25 was quite rigorous both before and after the rush-hour speed limit was lowered.
E) The number of people who drive on the M25 during rush hours did not increase after the rush-hour speed limit was lowered.

This is the ten billionth question about speed limits to appear on the LSAT. (That's a rough estimate.) Be careful not to bring in preconceptions from other speed limit questions you've seen on other LSATs. Even though the broad subject area is the same, the question is likely to be quite different.

This question presents a puzzling set of facts. The speed limit on a certain motorway was lowered, and rush-hour travel times went *down*. You probably would expect the opposite to be the case. How can this be explained?

Well, just like other similar questions we've encountered, there's no shortage of possible explanations. Maybe due to the speed limit lowering, some drivers are choosing not to take this road. Maybe they're driving on other roads, maybe they are taking the train—who knows? If any of these hypotheticals were true, the traffic could be thinned enough to lower commute times. (Remember, at rush hour, it's unlikely that the traffic is traveling anywhere near the speed limit, even the new lower limit.) Our advance answer is "some drivers are choosing not to drive on this road at rush hour."

A) This doesn't explain why rush hour commute times would have gone down after the speed limit was lowered. It's unsurprising that rush hour speeds are lower than speeds at other times of the day. We're looking for an "Aha!" moment and this is more like a "Duh" moment.
B) No explanation here either. Travel times during periods other than rush hour aren't relevant to the mystery of why rush hour commute times went down when the speed limit was lowered. Next contestant, please.
C) Thaaaaaaaat's it. If accidents were frequent and caused lengthy delays at rush hour, and if lowering the speed limit prevented those accidents, then lowering the speed limit might have decreased commute times. Because this answer makes me say "Oh, I get it now," and because the other answers do not, this must be right.
D) If enforcement was the same before and after the speed limit changed, then why did the commute times go down after the change?
E) If this said "decreased" instead of "did not increase" then this would be a good answer. But it doesn't. So it's not. Our answer is C.

QUESTION 13:

An art critic, by ridiculing an artwork, can undermine the pleasure one takes in it; conversely, by lavishing praise upon an artwork, an art critic can render the experience of viewing the artwork more pleasurable. So an artwork's artistic merit can depend not only on the person who creates it but also on those who critically evaluate it.

The conclusion can be properly drawn if which one of the following is assumed?

A) The merit of an artistic work is determined by the amount of pleasure it elicits.
B) Most people lack the confidence necessary for making their own evaluations of art.
C) Art critics understand what gives an artwork artistic merit better than artists do.
D) Most people seek out critical reviews of particular artworks before viewing those works.
E) The pleasure people take in something is typically influenced by what they think others feel about it.

As you may have noticed, I hate questions about art criticism. Unfortunately, they're all over the LSAT. Because I know this going in, I have to turn up my level of effort to eleven before diving in. If you know a certain topic really bothers you, it might be worth taking a five second time-out before you start the question. Close your eyes if you need to. Take a couple deep breaths, then begin. Once you begin, strongly focus your effort on trying to discern the main point of the speaker. If you can at least get the main point, you're well on the way toward coming up with a credible answer no matter what type of question is asked.

The problem with the argument on Question 13, like so many arguments on the LSAT, is that it uses a brand new concept (here, "artistic merit") in the conclusion. What the hell *is* artistic merit? There's no definition in the argument. The argument has the following elements: First, the premise that says art critics can make you enjoy a work of art less by ridiculing it. Second, the premise that says art critics can make you enjoy a work of art more by praising it. From these two premises, the author concludes that a work of art's *artistic merit* can depend on critics.

The question asks us to identify an additional premise that, if added to the existing premises, would make the argument logically sound. Essentially, we need something to build a bridge so that the speaker doesn't have to make a logical leap. If you practice enough on the LSAT, you can get scary good at this. My advance answer here is: "Anything that changes anyone's perception of something also changes that thing's merit." It's very broad and powerful, and that's okay on a sufficient-assumption question. If this advance answer is true, it makes the conclusion true, because it links the first parts of the premise with the concepts of the conclusion. That's what we need to do here.

A) This seems like it would do it. We have a premise that says art critics are capable of changing the amount of pleasure a piece of artwork elicits. If we accept A as true, then art critics are capable of changing the merit of an artistic work. This is a solid answer.
B) This is nowhere near as good as A, so let's eliminate it. This says nothing about artistic merit, which is key here, so it can't be the answer.
C) This at least has the words "artistic merit" but it doesn't connect the premises properly to the conclusion. Understanding artistic merit is not the issue. *Affecting* artistic merit is the issue. This is out.
D) Again, this says nothing about artistic merit, so it can't be the answer.
E) Again, nothing about artistic merit. A, which matched the advance answer closely, is our answer.

QUESTION 14:

The number of automobile thefts has declined steadily during the past five years, and it is more likely now than it was five years ago that someone who steals a car will be convicted of the crime.

Which one of the following, if true, most helps to explain the facts cited above?

A) Although there are fewer car thieves now than there were five years ago, the proportion of thieves who tend to abandon cars before their owners notice that they have been stolen has also decreased.
B) Car alarms are more common than they were five years ago, but their propensity to be triggered in the absence of any criminal activity has resulted in people generally ignoring them when they are triggered.
C) An upsurge in home burglaries over the last five years has required police departments to divert limited resources to investigation of these cases.
D) Because of the increasingly lucrative market for stolen automobile parts, many stolen cars are quickly disassembled and the parts are sold to various buyers across the country.
E) There are more adolescent car thieves now than there were five years ago, and the sentences given to young criminals tend to be far more lenient than those given to adult criminals.

Here we have an unsurprising correlation: Automobile thefts have declined at the same time as conviction rates for auto theft have gone up. There's no conclusion here, we're just asked to explain the facts we were given. Maybe the increasing conviction rates actually caused the declining rate of auto theft. Perhaps there's a new district attorney in the area, who has been more effective at getting convictions. That would explain why the conviction rates have been going up. And maybe word has been getting around that the new DA means business on car thefts, so the number of people taking the risk of stealing cars has declined. This isn't the only explanation, but this is one we can take with us as we venture into the answer choices.

A) If there are fewer car thieves, this would explain why there are fewer car thefts. And if the people who do steal cars are dumb enough to hold on to them long enough for the owners to realize they've gone missing, then they'll probably get caught more often, which would presumably lead to more convictions. So this is a pretty good answer.
B) This does explain why car thefts have gone down, but it wouldn't explain why conviction rates have gone up.
C) This wouldn't explain why car thefts have declined, and also wouldn't explain why conviction rates for car thefts have increased—in fact, it would make that circumstance seem very unlikely. This is a terrible answer.
D) This wouldn't explain why car thefts have declined, and would make the convictions seem less likely as well.
E) Not sure how more adolescent car thieves would lead to less car thefts. A higher conviction rate maybe, since adolescent car thieves might be really bad at it. But it's not solid enough to beat out our previous choice. Our answer is A.

QUESTION 15:

Legislator: My staff conducted a poll in which my constituents were asked whether they favor high taxes. More than 97 percent answered "no." Clearly, then, my constituents would support the bill I recently introduced, which reduces the corporate income tax.

The reasoning in the legislator's argument is most vulnerable to criticism on the grounds that the argument

A) fails to establish that the opinions of the legislator's constituents are representative of the opinions of the country's population as a whole
B) fails to consider whether the legislator's constituents consider the current corporate income tax a high tax
C) confuses an absence of evidence that the legislator's constituents oppose a bill with the existence of evidence that the legislator's constituents support that bill
D) draws a conclusion that merely restates a claim presented in support of that conclusion
E) treats a result that proves that the public supports a bill as a result that is merely consistent with public support for that bill

The legislator might want to look into the details of his poll before he leaps to any conclusions. Did his staffers poll his constituents about whether they were in favor of high taxes *for themselves*? Or whether they were in favor of high taxes *for corporations*? (One might imagine that more than three percent of the population holds the view that corporations should be heavily taxed.) We don't know exactly what the constituents were asked, and that's a problem. My advance answer is: "The legislator has concluded that her constituents are in favor of reducing taxes for corporations based on data that might indicate that they're in favor of reducing taxes for themselves."

A) The legislator only concludes that her constituents will favor a certain policy, not the entire country. So A is irrelevant.
B) I don't love this answer, but here's a case for it: The public did say that they are opposed to "high taxes." But because the poll didn't specifically define what a "high tax" is (a personal income tax? A corporate income tax?), we don't know whether the public considers the corporate income tax a high tax. I usually don't like to take this many words to explain my correct answer, so I'll only pick this one if everything else is terrible.
C) This is a different flaw. This would be the answer if the legislator had said, "My constituents haven't written me letters saying they don't want corporate taxes decreased, therefore they *do* want corporate taxes decreased." But that's not what the argument says, so this can't be right.
D) This would be the correct answer if the legislator had made an argument similar to "In the Bible, it says every word in the Bible is true. Therefore every word in the Bible is true." That's not what the argument does though. Hopefully E looks good.
E) The poll actually doesn't prove that the public supports the bill, since we don't know exactly what the poll asked the public. So this can't be the answer. All the answers here are bad. After reconsidering them, B is the only one I can really make any kind of reasonable case for. So even though I don't love it, B is our answer.

QUESTION 16:

Many nursing homes have prohibitions against having pets, and these should be lifted. The presence of an animal companion can yield health benefits by reducing a person's stress. A pet can also make one's time at a home more rewarding, which will be important to more people as the average life span of our population increases.

Which one of the following most accurately expresses the conclusion drawn in the argument above?

A) As the average life span increases, it will be important to more people that life in nursing homes be rewarding.
B) Residents of nursing homes should enjoy the same rewarding aspects of life as anyone else.
C) The policy that many nursing homes have should be changed so that residents are allowed to have pets.
D) Having a pet can reduce one's stress and thereby make one a healthier person.
E) The benefits older people derive from having pets need to be recognized, especially as the average life span increases.

As you read, you may have noticed that this argument doesn't seem to discuss any of the potential negatives of allowing pets in nursing homes. Are nursing-home patients susceptible to diseases carried by cats? (Toxoplasmosis, anyone? Look it up on Wikipedia if you want a mind-blowing study break—particularly the behavioral effects.) Would dogs tear up the rugs, thereby increasing facility costs? Would pot-bellied pigs get in the way of doctors and nurses trying to perform critical duties? If so, then maybe we shouldn't allow pets in nursing homes after all.

The question makes all of the potential weakeners irrelevant, since all it does is ask for the conclusion of the argument. This question is incredibly easy, having argued the way we just did. The (potentially ridiculous) conclusion of the argument is that pets should be allowed in nursing homes. We don't need to spend one second on any answer that doesn't say exactly that.

A) Nope, we're looking for "pets should be allowed in nursing homes." This was one of the reasons why, but it wasn't the conclusion.
B) Still no. Plus this wasn't even mentioned in the argument.
C) Yep, looks good.
D) Nope. We needed, and have already found, "pets should be allowed in nursing homes." This was one of the reasons why, but it wasn't the conclusion.
E) The argument didn't say the benefits of pets "should be recognized," it said specific policies should be changed. C is our answer.

QUESTION 17:

Near many cities, contamination of lakes and rivers from pollutants in rainwater runoff exceeds that from industrial discharge. As the runoff washes over buildings and pavements, it picks up oil and other pollutants. Thus, water itself is among the biggest water polluters.

The statement that contamination of lakes and rivers from pollutants in rainwater runoff exceeds that from industrial discharge plays which one of the following roles in the argument?

A) It is a conclusion for which the claim that water itself should be considered a polluter is offered as support.
B) It is cited as evidence that pollution from rainwater runoff is a more serious problem than pollution from industrial discharge.
C) It is a generalization based on the observation that rainwater runoff picks up oil and other pollutants as it washes over buildings and pavements.
D) It is a premise offered in support of the conclusion that water itself is among the biggest water polluters.
E) It is stated to provide an example of a typical kind of city pollution.

I hate trite arguments like this. "Water itself is a water polluter." Oooh, how clever. The LSAT seems to have quite a lot of arguments like this, where the speaker concludes something pseudointellectual after making a silly error in logic. (Actually, *the world* seems to have quite a lot of arguments like this.) Here, the error in logic is in saying that water is a polluter simply because rainwater can carry pollutants. The rainwater didn't cause those pollutants—the polluters put them in the rainwater! That's like you poisoning my drink, dumping my drink back into the punch bowl, and blaming the punch for poisoning everyone.

The question asks us to identify the role played in the argument by the statement that contamination from rainwater runoff exceeds that of industrial discharge. My advance answer is "the author used that statement to provide evidence that rain can carry a lot of pollutants, in order to then stupidly conclude that rainwater is a polluter."

A) I stopped reading this after "it is a conclusion." The statement was *not* a conclusion, it was a premise. This is out.
B) The argument never said that rainwater runoff contamination is a more serious problem than industrial discharge. The argument takes no position on what is serious and what isn't. So this is out.
C) The statement wasn't a "generalization" of anything. No thanks.
D) This very nearly matches my advance answer. Always a good thing.
E) The argument wasn't about typical types of city pollution. Answer D has perfectly described how and why this statement was used, so it's our answer.

QUESTION 18:

Wong: Although all countries are better off as democracies, a transitional autocratic stage is sometimes required before a country can become democratic.

Tate: The freedom and autonomy that democracy provides are of genuine value, but the simple material needs of people are more important. Some countries can better meet these needs as autocracies than as democracies.

Wong's and Tate's statements provide the most support for the claim that they disagree over the truth of which one of the following?

A) There are some countries that are better off as autocracies than as democracies.
B) Nothing is more important to a country than the freedom and autonomy of the individuals who live in that country.
C) In some cases, a country cannot become a democracy.
D) The freedom and autonomy that democracy provides are of genuine value.
E) All democracies succeed in meeting the simple material needs of people.

Wong says all countries would be better off as democracies, but says sometimes a "transitional autocratic stage" is required before a country can get to democracy. Tate says democracy "provides genuine value" but thinks some countries are better off as autocracies than democracies. So what they seem to disagree about is this: Tate thinks some countries are better off as autocracies in the long run, and Wong thinks every country would be better off as a democracy in the long run.

A) This seems to be it. Wong disagrees with this statement, but Tate agrees. That's the result we were looking for.
B) Wong takes no position on the importance of freedom and autonomy, so this can't possibly be the answer.
C) Neither speaker takes this position, so it can't be the answer.
D) Tate says yes to this, and Wong certainly doesn't say no. (Though he would probably agree if his thoughts on this were included.) Because Wong doesn't address this argument, this isn't their point of disagreement.
E) Wong takes no position on whether all democracies succeed in meeting simple material needs, so this can't be the answer. Let's go with A.

19

QUESTION 19:

Principle: When none of the fully qualified candidates for a new position at Arvue Corporation currently works for that company, it should hire the candidate who would be most productive in that position.

Application: Arvue should not hire Krall for the new position, because Delacruz is a candidate and is fully qualified.

Which one of the following, if true, justifies the above application of the principle?

A) All of the candidates are fully qualified for the new position, but none already works for Arvue.
B) Of all the candidates who do not already work for Arvue, Delacruz would be the most productive in the new position.
C) Krall works for Arvue, but Delacruz is the candidate who would be most productive in the new position.
D) Several candidates currently work for Arvue, but Krall and Delacruz do not.
E) None of the candidates already works for Arvue, and Delacruz is the candidate who would be most productive in the new position.

This is a tough one, and it might be easiest to solve by diagramming. Remember, I rarely diagram Logical Reasoning questions, and I only do it when I'm really confused. It can be pretty tough here to hold the principle and its application in my head, and to see the connection between the two statements. So let's use the conditional reasoning arrow (if ➞ then) to try to make some sense of it.

> Principle: No fully qualified internal candidates ➞ hire most productive candidate.
> Application: Delacruz is fully qualified ➞ do not hire Krall.

This helps us see it a little clearer, but there are still three steps to get all the way from the principle to the conclusion. To trigger the principle in the first place, we need to be sure there are no fully qualified internal candidates. This requires two things. First, Delacruz can't be internal (since she's fully qualified). Second, there can be no other fully qualified internal candidates. If these two things are true, then the sufficient condition of the principle is met and the company would therefore be forced to hire the most productive candidate. So the final thing we would need is another candidate, internal or external, who is more productive than Krall. If such a candidate exists, then we would be forced to hire that candidate instead of Krall.

Okay, that's a lot. To summarize, I think what we need to get from the principle to the application is "There are no fully qualified internal candidates, and there is another candidate more productive than Krall."

A) This wouldn't prevent us from hiring Krall. We have no idea whether Krall is the most productive candidate or not.
B) This wouldn't prevent us from hiring Krall either, because we might have fully qualified internal candidates.
C) Krall might be fully qualified, so this doesn't do it.
D) If we have several internal candidates, one of them might be qualified. So this doesn't do it.
E) This does it. If none of the candidates is internal, then we have to hire the most productive candidate. This person is Delacruz, so we shouldn't hire Krall. This was a very difficult question, but our answer is E.

The Science of Skipping

Unless you regularly score in the 170s, you probably should consider skipping a few questions as a strategy. This question makes me extremely uncomfortable. It takes me twice as long as a regular question, and I might miss it anyway. Only tackle questions like this if you're sure you're going to have plenty of time to finish the section. Otherwise, your time is best spent if you just bubble in a guess and move on, coming back to it later if you have time.

QUESTION 20:

Many important types of medicine have been developed from substances discovered in plants that grow only in tropical rain forests. There are thousands of plant species in these rain forests that have not yet been studied by scientists, and it is very likely that many such plants also contain substances of medicinal value. Thus, if the tropical rain forests are not preserved, important types of medicine will never be developed.

Which one of the following is an assumption required by the argument?

A) There are substances of medicinal value contained in tropical rain forest plants not yet studied by scientists that differ from those substances already discovered in tropical rain forest plants.
B) Most of the tropical rain forest plants that contain substances of medicinal value can also be found growing in other types of environment.
C) The majority of plant species that are unique to tropical rain forests and that have been studied by scientists have been discovered to contain substances of medicinal value.
D) Any substance of medicinal value contained in plant species indigenous to tropical rain forests will eventually be discovered if those species are studied by scientists.
E) The tropical rain forests should be preserved to make it possible for important medicines to be developed from plant species that have not yet been studied by scientists.

The logic here is pretty loose. According to the argument, it's "very likely" that the rain forests that have not yet been studied have many plants with substances of medicinal value. But "very likely" doesn't mean it's certain. From this shaky foundation, the passage makes an absolute conclusion: If the rain forests are not preserved, important types of medicine will never be developed. There are a couple problems with this: 1) The rain forests, even if preserved, might turn out not to have any plants of medicinal value. Or they could have plants of medicinal value, but the medicines produced by the plants might turn out to be medicines that have already been discovered in other ways. Like a painkiller that works, but isn't nearly as good as the hundreds of painkillers already on the market. 2) Scientists of the present or future might be able to synthesize the substances needed to develop the medicines even without finding them in the rainforest.

We're asked to find a Necessary Assumption, so let's restate the problems above as assumptions the author has made: 1) The author has assumed that the rain forests will have plants of medicinal value, and that these medicines are important because there aren't superior medicines already available. 2) The author has assumed that scientists of the present or future would not be able to synthesize the substances needed to develop the medicines without finding them in the rainforest.

A) This is similar to one of our predictions. The author has necessarily assumed that there must be substances of medicinal value in the unstudied rainforest that are *different* from what's already on the market. Note that if this answer is *not* true, the argument will fail. This is the definition of a Necessary Assumption.
B) If this were true it would weaken the author's argument, so it can't be the author's assumption.
C) This strengthens the author's argument, but it doesn't have to be true in order for the argument to be valid. So it's not an assumption *required* by the argument.
D) This is similar to C. It would strengthen the conclusion, but is too strong to be required by the argument. If "most" or even if "some" substances would eventually be discovered if studied by scientists, the conclusion that rain forests are necessary for the development of certain medicines would still stand. Therefore the phrase "any substance" in answer choice D is too strong to be an assumption required by the argument.
E) Nowhere does the author say we *should* preserve the rain forests. (The author says if we don't, then we'll miss out on discovering certain medicines, but doesn't go all the way to say we should preserve the rain forests.) Answer E states that we should, so it's out for going further than the author actually went. Our answer is A.

21

QUESTION 21:

In modern deep-diving marine mammals, such as whales, the outer shell of the bones is porous. This has the effect of making the bones light enough so that it is easy for the animals to swim back to the surface after a deep dive. The outer shell of the bones was also porous in the ichthyosaur, an extinct prehistoric marine reptile. We can conclude from this that ichthyosaurs were deep divers.

Which one of the following, if true, most weakens the argument?

A) Some deep-diving marine species must surface after dives but do not have bones with porous outer shells.
B) In most modern marine reptile species, the outer shell of the bones is not porous.
C) In most modern and prehistoric marine reptile species that are not deep divers, the outer shell of the bones is porous.
D) In addition to the porous outer shells of their bones, whales have at least some characteristics suited to deep diving for which there is no clear evidence whether these were shared by ichthyosaurs.
E) There is evidence that the bones of ichthyosaurs would have been light enough to allow surfacing even if the outer shells were not porous.

This argument extrapolates too broadly from one piece of data. It is true that whales have porous bones and are therefore able to dive deeply. But this is just one data point. The story about whales doesn't mean that every deep diver must have porous bones. (For example, submarines dive deeply and have no bones at all.) Further-more, not every creature with porous bones must dive deeply. Ichthyosaurs might have used their porous bones to dive deeply, or they might have stayed near the surface. There's too much that we just don't know.

A) This would weaken the argument somewhat, because it gives an example of a deep diver that does not have porous bones. But the answer is weak because of its use of the word "some." If we want to destroy the author's argument, we're ideally looking for a strong piece of evidence with which to attack.
B) It's not relevant whether most modern marine reptile species have porous bones. This neither strengthens nor weakens the argument.
C) This is better than A, because it says most (rather than some) non-diving species have porous bones. If this were true, then why would the author conclude that ichthyosaurs were deep divers because of their porous bones? C is the leader at this point.
D) The phrase "no clear evidence" kills this answer choice. Again, when we're at-tacking an argument, we want to be armed with evidence. At best, "no clear evidence" casts a small shadow over my opponent's case. We want to brutally bludgeon it, so this isn't the best answer.
E) This is either irrelevant or it is a strengthener. It's irrelevant because the ichthyo-saur *did* have porous bones, so we don't care what would have happened if its bones were not porous. Alternatively, we could consider this answer choice a strengthener because it's another data point in favor of ichthyosaurs being deep divers, which was the author's conclusion. In any case, this is definitely not a weakener. C is our answer.

QUESTION 22:

22

Librarian: Some argue that the preservation grant we received should be used to restore our original copy of our town's charter, since if the charter is not restored, it will soon deteriorate beyond repair. But this document, although sentimentally important, has no scholarly value. Copies are readily available. Since we are a research library and not a museum, the money would be better spent preserving documents that have significant scholarly value.

The claim that the town's charter, if not restored, will soon deteriorate beyond repair plays which one of the following roles in the librarian's argument?

A) It is a claim that the librarian's argument attempts to show to be false.
B) It is the conclusion of the argument that the librarian's argument rejects.
C) It is a premise in an argument whose conclusion is rejected by the librarian's argument.
D) It is a premise used to support the librarian's main conclusion.
E) It is a claim whose truth is required by the librarian's argument.

The librarian doesn't want to preserve the charter. He says "some argue" that it should be preserved, but then gives his own opinion that the charter has "no scholarly value." Then he goes further and says the money would be better spent preserving other documents. His main conclusion could be summarized as, "We shouldn't preserve the charter," or perhaps, "Instead of preserving the charter, we should preserve other documents."

The question points to a specific part of the librarian's argument, and asks us to determine what role this played. The phrase is "The town's charter, if not restored, will soon deteriorate beyond repair." This is certainly not the conclusion of the argument, since the librarian wants to go ahead and let the document deteriorate. Nor does this piece of information *support* the librarian's conclusion. So any answer choice that says this is a premise or the conclusion will be eliminated from contention. Our advance answer should be something like "The author acknowledges the truth of this statement, and recommends against taking action to stop it."

Vacating the Premises

On questions like this, always start by asking yourself whether the highlighted language is 1) the conclusion of the argument, 2) evidence used to support the conclusion (*i.e.*, a premise), or 3) something else. Sometimes this is enough to answer the question, and at the very least it will significantly narrow down the answer choices.

A) The librarian doesn't contest the reality that the charter is deteriorating. This can't be the answer.
B) Same as A. The librarian acknowledges the truth of the statement, rather than arguing against it.
C) Here we go. The argument the librarian rejects is "The town charter is deteriorating, therefore we should preserve it." The librarian acknowledges the truth of the premise "the town charter is deteriorating" but rejects the conclusion "we should preserve it." This has to be the correct answer.
D) It's not a premise of the librarian's argument. We can eliminate this one right off the bat.
E) Again, the statement is not used to support the librarian's conclusion. If the charter were not deteriorating, the librarian's conclusion "we should preserve other documents" would still stand. In fact, it would be strengthened. So this can't be the right answer. We're going with C.

QUESTION 23:

Columnist: Although much has been learned, we are still largely ignorant of the intricate interrelationships among species of living organisms. We should, therefore, try to preserve the maximum number of species if we have an interest in preserving any, since allowing species toward which we are indifferent to perish might undermine the viability of other species.

Which one of the following principles, if valid, most helps to justify the columnist's argument?

A) It is strongly in our interest to preserve certain plant and animal species.
B) We should not take any action until all relevant scientific facts have been established and taken into account.
C) We should not allow the number of species to diminish any further than is necessary for the flourishing of present and future human populations.
D) We should not allow a change to occur unless we are assured that that change will not jeopardize anything that is important to us.
E) We should always undertake the course of action that is likely to have the best consequences in the immediate future.

Rearranging the argument a bit for clarity, the logic here proceeds as follows:

1) We are largely ignorant of the interrelationships among species.
2) Allowing species toward which we are indifferent to perish might undermine the viability of other species. (Here, to make the story easier to understand, I'm picturing a species of brown slug that most people probably wouldn't care about. If we let the slug go extinct, we might later discover that the bald eagle depended on this brown slug somehow, and we'd end up losing the bald eagle, which people do care about.)
3) Therefore (conclusion), if we have an interest in preserving any species—the bald eagle, for example—we should try to preserve the maximum number of species (not just the bald eagle, but also brown slugs, *etcetera*).

I'm not sure what the weakness is in this argument. But one part we definitely don't have to worry about is whether or not we actually care about saving any species. This is irrelevant, because the conclusion was qualified with the phrase "*If* we care about preserving any species." We don't have to question whether we care, because the author's argument is only relevant if we do, in fact, care. So we can just go ahead and assume that we care. There will probably be an incorrect answer that is focused on this issue.

It's hard to say what the correct answer might look like here. Let's just try to find something that strengthens the argument.

A) This isn't relevant since the author qualified her conclusion by saying "if we have an interest." That simple phrase eliminates any concerns about whether we have an interest or not, per the discussion above. A doesn't help.
B) The author recommended action, and B can only be used to support inaction. So B isn't the answer.
C) This has "number of species" in it, which is in the conclusion, but it also has a bunch of nonsense about "human populations" that is disconnected from the argument. Can't see how this helps the argument.
D) This looks like the best answer. The author is worried about the unintended consequences of allowing brown slugs to perish. D says we shouldn't allow brown slugs to perish unless we're sure that brown slugs perishing won't jeopardize something important to us, like the bald eagle. This strengthens the argument (it's a generalized version of exactly what the argument says) so it sounds good.
E) There's nothing in the argument about the "immediate future." If anything, since it is about unintended consequences, the argument is probably more focused on the long run. E is therefore easily eliminated. Our answer is D.

QUESTION 24:

One is likely to feel comfortable approaching a stranger if the stranger is of one's approximate age. Therefore, long-term friends are probably of the same approximate age as each other since most long-term friendships begin because someone felt comfortable approaching a stranger.

The reasoning in the argument is flawed in that it

A) presumes, without warrant, that one is likely to feel uncomfortable approaching a person only if that person is a stranger
B) infers that a characteristic is present in a situation from the fact that that characteristic is present in most similar situations
C) overlooks the possibility that one is less likely to feel comfortable approaching someone who is one's approximate age if that person is a stranger than if that person is not a stranger
D) presumes, without warrant, that one never approaches a stranger unless one feels comfortable doing so
E) fails to address whether one is likely to feel comfortable approaching a stranger who is not one's approximate age

The first premise is "one is likely to feel comfortable approaching a stranger if the stranger is of one's approximate age." The second premise is "most long-term friendships begin because someone felt comfortable approaching a stranger." The conclusion is "long-term friends are probably of the same approximate age." This is stupid.

The problem with the reasoning, yet again, is that the author has confused a sufficient and a necessary condition. Yes, I will probably feel comfortable approaching a stranger of my age. But there is no premise that says I *won't* feel comfortable approaching a stranger of a *different* age. There could be many different things that make me feel comfortable around a stranger. Maybe you see that they're carrying golf clubs, and you're a golfer, so you strike up a conversation even though they're 20 years older or younger than you. Maybe you see them in an environment where you feel very comfortable, like your neighborhood coffee shop. There could be many (even infinite) reasons why someone would feel comfortable approaching a stranger. This argument has assumed that any sufficient condition is the only sufficient condition.

> ## Is That Really Necessary?
> Here's another example of this flaw: Bananas come from plants. Most foods that are good for you come from plants. So if a food is good for you, it's probably a banana.

We're not falling for it. By the time you're ready to take the test, this error should stick out like a sore thumb. This is a bellwether question: Your forward progress on the LSAT critically depends on understanding this point. If you don't get it, please ask me to explain it again (fox.edit@gmail.com).

A) The argument presumes that people only feel comfortable with strangers of the same age. This answer choice gets it backward and upside-down. Next, please.
B) This would be the answer if the argument was, "Most banks offer free checking accounts, therefore this bank offers free checking accounts." This isn't what we're looking for.
C) This answer choice was professionally written to waste our time. Remember the nonsense milkshake? Here's another. It takes key words from the argument and mixes them up, somewhat ridiculously, into a terrible answer choice. The argument is not about relative comfort with strangers versus nonstrangers. We can move right along to D.
D) This answer is too strong, in that the argument doesn't say that people never approach strangers they're not comfortable with. Furthermore, this answer is irrelevant, since the argument is only about relationships that do occur as a result of being comfortable with strangers. Let's keep looking.
E) Exactly. The argument assumes that there aren't alternate ways of feeling comfortable with strangers. The only trick to this question is that the correct answer is buried at E. They key to answering this question in a timely fashion is having a very strong advance answer that will allow you to dismiss the incorrect answer choices quickly in search of The One. E is The One.

25

QUESTION 25:

There can be no individual freedom without the rule of law, for there is no individual freedom without social integrity, and pursuing the good life is not possible without social integrity.

The conclusion drawn above follows logically if which one of the following is assumed?

A) There can be no rule of law without social integrity.
B) There can be no social integrity without the rule of law.
C) One cannot pursue the good life without the rule of law.
D) Social integrity is possible only if individual freedom prevails.
E) There can be no rule of law without individual freedom.

As easy as it is to hate this type of question (legal philosophy, with undefined terms), it's also fairly easy if we take our time. Diagramming should be used sparingly on Logical Reasoning questions, but the terms here are so amorphous that I know immediately I'm going to guide our way with a diagram. If we're careful, we can almost always predict the correct answer before going to the answer choices. These questions are almost mathematical in nature, or like writing a computer program.

The conclusion is the first part of the first sentence, and we know this because the word "for" is used after it. "For" means "because," so usually anything that comes after "for" is a premise.

P1: Individual freedom ➡ social integrity (social integrity is necessary for individual freedom)
P2: Pursing good life ➡ social integrity (social integrity is necessary for pursuing the good life)
Conclusion: Individual freedom ➡ rule of law (rule of law is *necessary* for individual freedom)

How do we get from the premises to the conclusion? Looks like we can get there only through Premise 1. (Premise 2 seems unnecessary since the conclusion mentions individual freedom.) Our advance answer is "social integrity requires the rule of law." If true, then the logic of the whole argument would look like this:

Individual freedom ➡ social integrity ➡ rule of law

So let's go into this one keeping in mind both "social integrity requires the rule of law," and "without the rule of law, there can be no social integrity."

A) This is backward.
B) This is exactly what we predicted, so it's got to be the answer.
C) Normally you should engage with all five answer choices, but because this question type is so mathematical in nature, if one of the answer choices matches the answer you derived in your diagram, you're basically going to live or die with it. Scan through the remaining answers only to see if there's something that is almost an identical match to B. This isn't, so it's out.
D) It's not like B, so it's out.
E) Not like B either. Our answer is B.

26

QUESTION 26:

Economist: Countries with an uneducated population are destined to be weak economically and politically, whereas those with an educated population have governments that display a serious financial commitment to public education. So any nation with a government that has made such a commitment will avoid economic and political weakness.

The pattern of flawed reasoning in which one of the following arguments is most similar to that in the economist's argument?

A) Animal species with a very narrow diet will have more difficulty surviving if the climate suddenly changes, but a species with a broader diet will not; for changes in the climate can remove the traditional food supply.

B) People incapable of empathy are not good candidates for public office, but those who do have the capacity for empathy are able to manipulate others easily; hence, people who can manipulate others are good candidates for public office.

C) People who cannot give orders are those who do not understand the personalities of the people to whom they give orders. Thus, those who can give orders are those who understand the personalities of the people to whom they give orders.

D) Poets who create poetry of high quality are those who have studied traditional poetry, because poets who have not studied traditional poetry are the poets most likely to create something shockingly inventive, and poetry that is shockingly inventive is rarely fine poetry.

E) People who dislike exercise are unlikely to lose weight without sharply curtailing their food intake; but since those who dislike activity generally tend to avoid it, people who like to eat but dislike exercise will probably fail to lose weight.

Wow, this one is a doozy. If you've ever considered doing the questions out of order (back to front, for example), this question should disabuse you of that notion forever. Not only is it very long (it takes up its own column) but it's also full of double negatives, and therefore a pain in the ass to understand. I would guess that only about 40 percent of all test takers got this one right, and that includes those who outright guessed.

Once we wade through all the crap, the argument has a premise about countries with uneducated populations and a premise about countries with educated populations. The two premises really don't connect. Countries with uneducated populations are destined to be weak economically and politically, and countries with educated populations have governments that display a serious financial commitment to public education. That's nice, but it doesn't add up to much. The conclusion of the argument, however, tries to draw a connection: Any nation with a government that has made such a commitment will avoid economic and political weakness. This conclusion is not supported by the facts.

A similarly flawed argument, in real terms, would be "If you're not a cheetah, then you're slow, and if you are a cheetah, then you have spots. Therefore all animals with spots are fast."

This flaw, in the abstract, is "If not A, then B, and if A, then C. Therefore if C, then not B."

I'm looking for an argument that matches this flaw.

A) This argument begins "If A, then B, and if not A, then not B." This doesn't match our flaw, so it can be eliminated.

B) This matches exactly. If you're incapable of empathy (not A) then you're a bad candidate (B). If you do have empathy (A) then you're able to manipulate (C). Therefore people who can manipulate (C) are good candidates (not B).

C) This is "If not A, then not B, therefore if A, then B." It's a flaw, but it's not a matching flaw.

D) This is "If A then B, because if not B then C, and if C then D." Too many terms... this is out.

E) There is nothing here about people who like exercise, so I don't even have to bother with it. (The argument we are trying to match had two different, separate groups in it.) Our answer is B.

Don't waste too much time studying this question. There are much better uses of your time.

Epilogue

Whether you think the LSAT is easy or hard, you're right. Mindset is at least half the battle. What I do for a living is convince students that the test is actually quite a bit easier than they initially thought. Really, there are just three types of questions:

1) **Questions that are basically easy.** Example: The correlation-equals-causation flaw. Maybe you get these right away, or maybe they trip you up a few times, but after you've done a moderate amount of practice you'll see these questions coming a mile away. This is probably a quarter of the test.

2) **Questions that look hard on the surface, but eventually become very easy.** Example: Logic games that require you to understand complex rules and link them together. These will take a lot of practice, but you can become expert at them. This is probably half the test. If you master types one and two, you can score in the 160s.

3) **Questions that are actually hard.** Example: Very long match-the-pattern-of-reasoning questions. These questions are difficult even for experts, and they generally appear toward the end of each section. You can make them incredibly easy by skipping them outright and filling in an answer bubble at random. Or, you can get very good at types one and two so that you have plenty of extra time to devote to these questions. This is probably a quarter of the test. It's not the difference between going to law school and not going to law school, but it does impact what kinds of offers you'll receive.

Start with types one and two. Do a little bit every day. I've never met anyone who couldn't improve his or her LSAT score dramatically by following this simple plan. And as always, let me know if I can help: fox.edit@gmail.com.

APPENDIX:

Logical Reasoning Question Types

What you need to do first, foremost, and always is *argue with the speaker,* and you'll be fine no matter what type of question you're looking at.

But certain question types *do* prefer certain types of answers, so after you've already done your best to understand the argument, it's definitely useful to think about what type of question you're dealing with. Here are some of the common question types, and here's how I like to break them down:

Strategy of Argumentation: (Example: "Mal's response to Zoe proceeds by ... ")

Some questions of this type simply ask you to identify the type of reasoning used by an argument. In this case, you must find the answer choice that best describes the logic of the argument as a whole. Note that the correct answer will probably not contain any of the specific details from the argument. Instead, the answer will contain an abstract, or general, description of the method of argumentation used. Since there are frequently several different ways to abstractly describe an argument, it's difficult to predict the correct answer before looking at the answer choices.

A common variation on this type is a question that asks you to identify the role played in an argument by a particular phrase or sentence. **(Example: "Jayne's assertion that Vera is his most favorite gun plays which one of the roles in his argument?")** On these types of questions, I always ask myself, "Is it the main conclusion of the argument?" If the answer is no, then I ask a follow-up question: "Does it support the main conclusion of the argument?" Sometimes, you will be able to exactly predict the correct answer in advance. (You'll feel pretty awesome when this happens.) If not, then you will almost certainly be able to narrow down the answer choices by simply understanding whether the phrase in question was the conclu-

sion, a premise that supports the conclusion, or something else. Once you've got that down, you're in good shape.

Main Conclusion (Example: "Which one of the following most accurately expresses the conclusion of Wash's argument?")

Questions that ask you to identify the main conclusion are among the easiest questions on the LSAT, since you should always be looking for the conclusion of an argument anyway. (How can you be arguing with the speaker if you don't understand their main point?) On this type of question, you absolutely should predict the correct answer before looking at the answer choices. If you're having any trouble, try asking the speaker, "Why are you wasting my time with this?" to see if it helps you zero in on the speaker's main point.

Must Be True (Example: "Which one of the following must be true, if Kaylee's statements above are correct?")

This question type can be tricky when you first start studying for the LSAT, because you might be inclined to pass up answer choices that seem "too obvious." Don't do that! Be open to the possibility that you're actually plenty smart enough to punch this test in the face. On a question of this type, all you're looking for is the one answer that has been *proven* by the speaker's statements (and nothing more than the speaker's statements ... outside information is not allowed.) The correct answer does not have to be the speaker's main point, nor does the speaker's entire statement have to be related to the correct answer. If any part of the speaker's statement *proves* that an answer choice has to be true, then that's your answer. This question type is pretty easy once you get the hang of it.

A common variation on this type of question is the slightly more fluid, and therefore slightly trickier, question that asks you to find something that might not *necessarily* be true based on the given statement, but is at least partially supported by the statement. **(Example: "Which one of the following is most strongly supported by Kaylee's statements?")** The general idea is the same, and this is still a pretty manageable type of question. Pick the answer that is best supported by Kaylee's statement—and no more than Kaylee's statement. (Again, outside information is not allowed.) The correct answer here might not be *proven* true by what Kaylee has said, but ideally it will be pretty damn close to proven.

Agree/Disagree (Example: "Simon and River have committed to disagreeing on which of the following?")

This is another very manageable question type once you know what to look for. (Sensing a theme here? Practice, practice, practice and you'll be in good shape.) Here, we are asked to identify the answer that Simon and River have *actually, already, in their statements*, disagreed upon. Easily dismissed incorrect answer choices might give a statement that Simon and River agree on—there are usually one or two of these. But trickier incorrect answers will frequently be something that Simon and River *probably* disagree on. One common trap on this type of question is an answer choice that the second speaker clearly takes a position on, and which might seem contrary to the first speaker's position, but the first speaker didn't actually address. Don't fall for that crap! You should be able to show me, in Simon's statement, where he said "yes" to a particular answer choice, and then show me, in River's statement, where she said "no" to that same statement. Or vice versa.

A common variation on this type of question is a question that asks you to identify a statement that the two speakers *agree* on. This is easy, as long as you don't make the tragic mistake of reading too fast and thinking you're supposed to be looking for a point of disagreement. It's devastating when that happens.

Weaken (Example: "Which one of the following, if true, most weakens Shepherd Book's argument?")

My primary piece of advice on the Logical Reasoning is "always be attacking," no matter what type of question you're looking at. So a question that asks you to undermine an argument's reasoning shouldn't be too much of a problem. As you read each question, you should always be coming up with weakeners. For me, this takes the form of "Oh yeah,

well you're full of shit, because what about this? Or what about that? Or what about this other thing?" I'm constantly barraging the speaker with skepticism. Ideally, by the time the speaker comes around to his conclusion, I'm armed with at least a couple potential holes in the argument. The answer might very well be exactly one of these predictions, or it might be something similar. Even if it's not something I've already thought of, being in that skeptical state of mind helps me spot a kindred argument.

If you're having trouble on weaken questions, you probably aren't quite clear about what it means to "weaken" an argument on the LSAT. Here it is: You weaken an argument by showing that its evidence doesn't justify its conclusion. There are many ways to do this, but at a minimum you *must* know what the conclusion is, and you also must know what evidence was used to reach that conclusion.

Once you understand the argument, there are countless ways to attack it. Maybe Shepherd Book's premises simply don't add up to his conclusion, leaving a hole in the argument. Or maybe Shepherd Book's conclusion and his evidence can't simultaneously be true. Or maybe he made a sufficient vs. necessary error. (More on that ahead.) Maybe he made a correlation-equals-causation error. Pick the answer that, if true, causes the argument to be faulty, nonsensical, or just plain stupid. Ask yourself: "Which one of these facts, if I were an attorney arguing *against* Shepherd Book, would I most like to be true?"

Incorrect answer choices on Weaken questions will either strengthen the argument, or, more commonly, simply be irrelevant. One trap to look out for is an answer choice that seems to go against Shepherd Book's position, but doesn't really address his argument. (For example, if the Shepherd's argument was about one particular group of people, and the answer choice talks about a different group of people.)

Unlike Must Be True questions, it's totally acceptable to use outside information to answer a Weaken question.

Strengthen (Example: "Which one of the following, if true, most strengthens Shepherd Book's argument?")

Arguments can be strengthened in just as many ways as they can be weakened. You're really just doing the reverse of the process described above. Pick the answer that strengthens the connection between the premises and the conclusion. If there is a big hole in the argument, then fill that gap as best you can. The correct answer on this type of question won't always prove that the conclusion is true, but you should pick the one that gets you the furthest toward that goal. Ask yourself: "Which one of these facts, if I were an attorney *for* Shepherd Book, would I most like to be true?" Again, outside information is fully acceptable here.

Which Fact Would be Most Useful (Example: "Which one of the following would be most useful in determining the validity of Shepherd Book's claim?")

This isn't a very common type of question—it appears maybe once, on average, on each test. Each answer choice is itself a question, and you are asked to pick the one that has the most bearing on the argument. I find that if I read the argument to weaken (which I always do) then I can do a pretty good job of predicting what the missing information is. Ask yourself: "If I were a police officer evaluating Shepherd Book's story, which one of these questions would I ask?" Pick the question that, if answered one way, makes Shepherd guilty, but if answered another way, makes Shepherd innocent.

Necessary Assumptions (Example: "Which one of the following is an assumption on which Inara's argument depends?")

Note the subtle, but very important, distinction between this question type (Necessary Assumption) and the one that follows (Sufficient Assumption). The Necessary Assumption question means, "Which one of the following *must be true in order for Inara's argument to make sense*?" Pick the answer that, if untrue, would make Inara's argument ridiculous. Another way of thinking about this is "Which one of the following is an assumption that Inara actually made?" Avoid answers that are stronger, or more absolute, than the minimum required for Inara's conclusion to make sense. If Badger is on the planet Persephone, and Inara concludes that Badger is a dick, then she has necessarily assumed that at least one person on Persephone is a dick. She has *not* assumed that everyone on Persephone is a dick.

Sufficient Assumptions (Example: "Which one of the following, if assumed, would allow Inara's conclusion to be properly drawn?")

This question means, "Which one of the following, *if true, would prove Inara's conclusion*? Pick the answer that, if true, would force Inara's conclusion to be true. Here, unlike a Necessary Assumption question, there is no limit on the strength or absoluteness of the correct answer. In fact, the bigger the better. If Inara had concluded that Badger is a dick, the correct answer might be something extreme like "Everyone on Persephone is a dick" (if Badger is on Persephone) or even simply "everyone is a dick." (Am I the only one who has days like that?) If either of these statements were true, then Inara's conclusion would be proven. It might be useful to think of Sufficient Assumption questions as "Super-Strengthen" questions. Conversely, Necessary Assumption questions might be considered more closely related to Weaken questions, because you're picking the answer that, if false, would destroy the argument.

Applying a Principle that is Given (Example: "Which one of the following would be a proper application of the principle stated by Niska?")

Here, all you have to do is 1) understand the principle and 2) pick the answer that conforms to the principle. Suppose Niska's principle is "I never let anyone damage my reputation without getting revenge." Incorrect answers might include situations where people damage Niska's reputation without Niska then getting revenge, or Niska getting revenge on people who did not damage his reputation in the first place. The correct answer would most likely include someone doing something damaging to Niska's reputation, and Niska then exacting his revenge.

Identifying a Guiding Principle (Example: "Which one of the following principles best justifies Niska's actions?")

This is the reverse of the "Applying a Principle" question discussed above. The prompt would include a story, and you would be asked to identify a principle that would "justify" or "make acceptable" Niska's actions. You're distilling the essence of the story on these questions. For example, the story might include someone damaging Niska's reputation, and Niska then getting revenge. The correct answer would say something like "It is always acceptable to get revenge if someone damages your reputation."

Flaw (Example: "Which one of the following illustrates a flaw in Saffron's reasoning?")

With enough practice, you should get really good at these questions. They are similar to Weaken questions, in that you're asked to identify a problem with the argument. Flaw questions make actual errors of logic. Suppose Saffron had attacked the character of a speaker, rather than addressing the speaker's facts and reasoning. This is the "source attack," or "ad hominem" flaw. The same flaws appear over and over and over on the LSAT, and with practice you will start to see them coming a mile away. (You're not going to fall for the same bad logic more than two or three times, right?) There are way too many flaws to fit in this appendix, but Wikipedia's "fallacy" page is a great resource if you feel like doing some reading.

Matching Pattern (Example: "Which one of the following arguments is most similar to the reasoning in Patience's argument above?")

These are among the most time consuming and difficult questions on the LSAT. Most students (let's say, roughly, anyone regularly scoring 160 or below on their practice tests) should be skipping these questions and coming back to them at the end of the section if there's time. This is especially true on the extremely long Matching Pattern questions. Why would we waste our time on a question that takes up its own column on the page, when we could answer two other questions in the same amount of time? Make sure you've harvested all the low-hanging fruit before you break out the 40-foot ladder.

Because Matching Pattern questions are so tough to nail and are often time-consuming, I end up trusting my gut more than anything else. First, I read the argument carefully and see if I can get a feel for the general pattern of reasoning. Then, I ask myself if the logic in the argument is generally good or generally bad. If the logic in the argument is good, then the logic in the correct answer should also be good. If the logic is generally bad, then the logic in the correct answer should also be bad—and bad in the exact same way. If the beginning of an answer choice is wrong, I won't even bother reading the rest of it. (Example: The given argument says nothing about cause and effect, and an answer choice starts out with something about causation.) Sometimes it's impossible to be 100 percent sure that I have chosen the correct answer on a Matching Pattern question. I'm OK with that. But that's also why they're good candidates to skip.

Matching Flaw (Example: "Which one of the following arguments is most similar to the flawed pattern of reasoning used by Patience?")

This is a slightly easier variation on the Matching Pattern question, because there is something specifically *wrong* with the argument. The correct answer will have the exact same flaw. Make sure you identify the flaw before you look at the answer choices.

Explanation (Example: "Which of the following, if true, contributes most to an explanation of the puzzling situation described above?")

These questions are fun, because they set up a mystery and then ask you to explain that mystery. For example, the argument might go something like "*Firefly* was a bitchin' space western TV series on Fox. The show had great characters, fun stories, and a rabid fan base. Fox canceled the show after one season." Make sure you understand the mystery before looking at the answer choices. Why the hell would Fox cancel a show with so much going for it? That's the mystery.

The correct answer on an Explanation question should, obviously, *explain* that mystery. The correct answer should, ideally, make you say "Aha!" One type of common incorrect answer for an Explanation question is something simply irrelevant, like "Fox is owned by Rupert Murdoch." That's true, but it doesn't explain anything. Another type of common incorrect answer on an Explanation question will actually make the mystery even harder to understand, like "Fox executives claim to want to produce great shows." Here, the correct answer could be something like "Fox executives don't like shows with great characters." Or "Fox executives don't like fans." Or something broader, like "Fox executives are just plain stupid."

About the Author

Nathan Fox didn't figure out what he wanted to be when he grew up until he was well past grown. He has been an undergrad economics student, a stockbroker, a half-assed computer programmer, a project manager, a product manager (and he can't really tell you the difference between the two), a graduate journalism student, an editor, a graduate business student, a law student, and finally an LSAT teacher. He still has nightmares about the first nine things, and loves the last thing so much that he can't believe he gets paid to do it.

He encourages you to keep searching until you find the thing that 1) you are good at, 2) you enjoy doing, and 3) you can get paid to do. There is no reason to settle for less.

Acknowledgments

This book, and Fox Test Prep, would never have existed without the constant love, support, patience, and encouragement of Christine. The power of having somebody who believes in you (especially someone so incredibly sweet) cannot be overstated. I'd still be on the couch playing Mario Kart without her—she's a wonderful reason to finally grow up.

Anyone can put their hands all over your crappy manuscript and make it clean, concise, and consistent. Mike Krolak is the rare editor/publisher who can do all that while also, miraculously, making it sound more like you.

Christine, Mike, and the rest of my friends and family have tolerated endless whining as I've tried degree after degree, career after career, and bitched the entire way. But now I've finally found my niche, and I couldn't be happier. If everyone had such a strong support network, perhaps more people would be lucky enough to do the same.

Finally, I owe an immense debt of gratitude to the hundreds of LSAT students who have helped me hone my LSAT techniques and explanations in the classroom. A wise teacher told me, as I was very nervously anticipating my first class, to tell the truth to my students even when I didn't know the right answer. I walked into class the next day and opened with "I'm not supposed to tell you this, but this is the very first class I have ever taught." I expected them to demand refunds. Instead, I was hit with an unexpected wave of warmth and acceptance.

I have yet to teach a single class without making at least one stupid mistake and having a student patiently tell me how to fix it. The good parts of this book are the result of those corrections, and the rest of them are just errors that my students have yet to point out to me. Thank you for making the classroom feel like home. Thank you for not complaining when I drop far too many obscenities in class. And thank you for letting me regale you with my half-baked analogies between golf and the LSAT. I don't know how you make it through my four-hour classes with such grace—it feels like I should be paying you.

Made in the USA
Lexington, KY
09 August 2012